LEWIS
AGONISTES

D1562683

LOUIS MARKOS

LEWIS
AGONISTES

HOW C.S. LEWIS CAN TRAIN US TO WRESTLE WITH THE MODERN AND POSTMODERN WORLD

BROADMAN
&HOLMAN
PUBLISHERS

Nashville, Tennesse

Ten-digit ISBN: 0-8054-2778-3
Thirteen-digit ISBN: 978-0-8054-2778-3

Published by Broadman & Holman Publishers,
Nashville, Tennessee

Dewey Decimal Classification: 261
Subject Heading: LEWIS, C.S.—CRITICISM \ CHRISTIAN
SOCIOLOGY \ SOCIAL CONFLICT

Scripture quotations are taken from the *Holman Christian Standar
Bible*® Copyright © 1999, 2000, 2002, 2004 by Holman Bible
Publishers. Used by permission.

.

5 6 7 8 9 10   09 08 07 06

for
my wife, Donna,
for wrestling with me in love

Pierre Matta and Dan Stickle,
for wrestling with me in friendship

and Harold Raley,
for wrestling with me in the halls of the academy

Contents

Preface

In the thirty-second chapter of Genesis, a trembling and chastened Jacob prepares to meet the older brother whose birthright and inheritance he had stolen. As he prays deep into the night, a man appears and wrestles with him until dawn. But when the first rays of the sun begin to appear on the horizon and the man realizes that Jacob will not let him go, he touches Jacob's hip, miraculously ripping it from its socket. Now incapacitated, Jacob cannot hope to overcome his foe, and yet, in desperation, he grabs hold of him, swearing that he will not release him until he bestows on Jacob a blessing. The man agrees, but his blessing will prove to be a strange one: a change of name that will carry with it as well a change of destiny. Henceforth, his name will be Isra-el, the one who wrestles with God. For the man with whom he wrestled was none other than the Lord himself, and the people to be born out of Jacob's loins will be no ordinary people. They will be one of a hundred people groups, yet somehow forever distinct—not just pawns in the great and bloody clash of ancient civilizations, but battlers themselves, rising somehow above them all. Not to them will be allowed the luxury of blending into the cultures that surround them; they will carry on an endless *agon*—a wrestling match between the physical and the spiritual, the earthly and the heavenly. And out of their loins would, in turn, rise another group of wrestlers, a group devoted to a great and mystic call: to be in the world but not of it. For hundreds of years, the struggling Christian church grappled with the accepted practices of the Roman culture around them.

But a day came when that same Church rose to become itself the central power, and thus was ushered in a new challenge: the temptation to embrace complacency, to lay down the cultural gauntlet, to end the agon. Perhaps no age has so dulled the edge of the Christian agon as a time in which modern and postmodern ideologies have proven so monolithic, so all-embracing that most Christians cannot step back far enough to get the proper perspective needed for a full and effective critique. Thankfully, though, our age also produced one of Christianity's greatest wrestlers, a man whose vision allowed him to pierce through the modern and postmodern tree to examine the roots that sustain it. That man was C. S. Lewis, a man who richly deserves the epithet, Agonistes (the wrestler; pronounced a-go-NISS-tees). Just as Samson (about whom John Milton wrote a play entitled *Samson Agonistes*) wrestled both with his internal temptations and the external Philistines, so Lewis wrestled first with his own inner prejudices against Christianity and then carried that wrestling into the outer world of modern and postmodern ideas.

In the five sections that make up this book, I shall follow Lewis Agonistes as he carries his agon on to five of the most contested battlefields of the twentieth century: 1) science, 2) the New Age, 3) evil and suffering, 4) the arts, and 5) heaven and hell. In each section, I shall, after stating and defining the challenge, show how Lewis answers that challenge both by means of a reactive defense that takes us back to an older, medieval countervision and a proactive offense that looks ahead to a new synthesis of ancient and modern.

Before engaging in this fivefold struggle, however, I will pause to consider the major events and people in Lewis's life that prepared him to become the great wrestler of our age. Numerous excellent biographies already exist of Lewis's life (the best of them being *Jack* by George Sayers), and so I shall not attempt to offer an exhaustive overview of his life and letters. Rather, I shall keep my focus on the struggle between the rational and the intuitive, the modern and the medieval that shaped Lewis's unique journey of faith and helped mold him into an apologist of prodigious and diverse talents. Once this has been established, I will then move directly into the challenges themselves.

The first challenge (purely a modernist one) comes from science with its dismissal of supernatural Christianity and its pervasive evolutionary mind-set. This paradigm is so ubiquitous as to be invisible; it encompasses not only the legacy of Marx, Freud, Darwin, and Nietzsche, but takes in anthropology, higher criticism, and the dethroning of Homer by classicists. In this arena, Lewis shall unmask and disarm the modernist project, offering both a list of essential things that could not have evolved and a wider vision of miracles that transcends the narrow limits of inductive science.

The New Age, in part a postmodern reaction to the excesses of modernism, offers not only a theological challenge to Christianity but threatens to compete with her for the soul of America's youth. With Lewis as a guide, I shall argue that if we shift our focus to the New Age as a type of yearning in the modern soul for a return to a meaningful universe, to a cosmos filled with its Father's presence, then the New Age becomes not a threat but a challenge—an invitation for the church to widen its reach, to identify and speak to yearnings that point back finally not to pantheism and pagan revelry but to a Triune, Incarnate God who created the cosmos and who often reveals himself through it.

The third section shall take up an issue that believers and nonbelievers have struggled with since time began: the problem of evil and suffering. Though this issue is not unique to modernity-postmodernity, I shall show how it has been influenced and exacerbated by the liberal Victorian faith that man, through technology, social reform, and education can build a utopia free from ignorance, poverty, and pain, and by a concomitant rise in a deterministic view of history and of mankind. In wrestling with this issue, I shall reference Lewis's thoughts on 1) what he calls God's free will experiment, 2) his unique meditations on the nature of creation, the fall, and disobedience, and 3) his notion that pain is God's megaphone to rouse a deaf world. This section will close with a look at how Lewis reassessed his earlier view on pain after experiencing his own personal loss, the death of his wife Joy.

Fourth, the postmodern breakdown of signifier and signified has left language and the arts powerless to embody the kinds of truths that lie at the heart of orthodox Christianity. After explaining in lay terms how deconstruction has threatened the very meaning of meaning, I shall argue that the church, far from answering this challenge, has been an unwitting accomplice in the postmodern assault on the meaningfulness of the arts. With the help of Lewis, I shall then attempt to fashion an aesthetics of incarnation, one that will not only speak to the potential of the arts to bear a heavy weight of meaning but that will champion the arts as a far greater friend than foe to the beleaguered apologist living in a postmodern world.

The final section will take up the issue of heaven and hell and how these central beliefs have been attacked both by modernism (with its rejection of hell as unjust and non-egalitarian and its consignment of heaven to wish fulfillment) and postmodernism (with its relativizing of the whole notion of sin and its suggestion that heaven and hell are merely states of mind). In answering this modern demythologizing of the afterlife, I shall discuss Lewis's concept of the psychology of sin: that hell is always something we choose and that it is less an end point than a process by which the damned soul slowly dehumanizes itself. I shall show how Lewis, in mock-Freudian style, offers a series of case studies through which he explores the various ways in which sin and idolatry slowly strip away our humanity. More generally, I shall demonstrate, through a wrestling with Lewis's ideas, that heaven and hell can be defended in such a way as to both stay true to the orthodox Christian position and appeal to thinkers raised in a postmodern age.

It is my firm belief that if Christians of today are to make full use of Lewis's legacy in taking up the specific challenges of their moment in history, then they will need a resource that does three basic things: 1) explains in lay terms exactly *what* the challenges of modernity-postmodernity are and how these challenges surface in various areas; 2) forges the arguments, illustrations, and overall vision of the fictional and nonfictional writings of C. S. Lewis into weapons with which the Christian can do battle; 3) encourages and enables its readers to become participants themselves in the agon, or wrestling match, of the twenty-first century.

Lewis Agonistes attempts to do all these things, and something more: It makes its readers work in the same way that Lewis's books make them work. That is to say, it will force them to rethink and re-examine ideas that they have long taken for granted and to delve down to the assumptions on which they rest. Our age, thankfully, has already been provided with a number of fine books that help us to understand what Lewis said and what he meant by what he said. It is my intent to go beyond analysis: to not only wrestle *through* Lewis but *alongside* him as well. There will, therefore, be long passages in this book where Lewis's name is not mentioned. In such passages, I will either be working through an examination of the precise challenges leveled by the modern and postmodern world (partly in preparation for Lewis's entrance into the arena), or constructing an argument of my own that is guided by Lewis's method and approach and that attempts to carry that approach into the twenty-first century.

Thus far, I have spoken as if the readers of *Lewis Agonistes* will be all Christian believers. It is my hope that it will also attract open-minded theists (and even atheists) who are troubled by some of the more radical aspects of modernity-postmodernity and who still respect the Western tradition and the central part that Christianity and the Bible have played in that tradition. All of us, whatever our religious beliefs, have a stake in our modern-postmodern culture and the consequences that rise up out of that culture. May Lewis prove a worthy guide as we assess what those consequences are and will be, and in so doing, challenge ourselves to question again beliefs and assumptions we have long taken for granted.

—∞—

This book had a somewhat interesting genesis. It began as an article that I wrote for the April 21, 2001 issue of *Christianity Today* ("Myth Matters: How C. S. Lewis bequeathed us a method and a language for sharing the gospel with the modern and postmodern world"); in that article I laid out the core theses that underlie chapters 2, 3, and 5 (on science, the New Age, and the arts). The following year, I converted these three theses into three plenary addresses (collectively titled *Lewis Agonistes: Wrestling with the Modern and Postmodern World*), which I delivered at The Fourth Annual C. S. Lewis and the Inklings Conference held at Amarillo College in April of 2002. At that time, the addresses were merely outlines from which I spoke extemporaneously. From these outlines, I constructed chapters 2, 3, and 5, and then went on to add the material found in chapters 1, 4, and 6, always holding to the basic method and focus that I had laid out in the *Christianity Today* article and in my addresses. As for the text of "Myth Matters," I have incorporated much of it into this book, along with a second brief article published in the October 1, 2001 issue of *Christianity Today* ("Poetry Phobic: Why evangelicals should love language that is 'slippery'"). Portions of chapter 3 borrow significant passages from an article I published in the spring 2001 issue of *Mythlore* ("Apologist for the Past: The Medieval Vision of C. S. Lewis's Space Trilogy and Chronicles of Narnia"). Finally, scattered portions of this book reflect much of the research I did in putting together a twelve-lecture series entitled *The Life and Writings of C. S. Lewis.* This series was produced by the Teaching Company (1-800-TEACH12; www.teach12.com) and is available in both audio and video. I also relied on some of the research I did for a second series (twenty-four lectures) produced with The Teaching Company: *Plato to Postmodernism: Understanding the Essence of Literature and The Role of the Author.* (Needless to say, the research I did for these two series was itself based on research I did for my classes at Houston Baptist University and for several scattered talks and papers.) I would like to gratefully acknowledge all of the above groups and to thank them for the interest they have shown in my work.

On a more personal note, I would like to acknowledge the love and support of my wife, Donna, my son, Alex, my daughter, Stacey, my parents, Tom and Angie Markos, my brother, George Markos, and my in-laws, Don and Lois Van Lare. Second, thanks is due to the administration of Houston Baptist University, particularly to my present and former deans, Dr. James Taylor and Dr. Harold Raley, and chair, Dr. Phyllis Thompson, for their support and encouragement. Third, eternal gratitude to my students (especially my English majors) who have inspired me with their willingness to integrate their faith and their love of literature. Among the many, I must at least mention a few: Paula Behrens, Jennifer Bishop, Terry Bohannon, Bill Brewer, Brandy Brooks, Elizabeth Farrar, Jennifer Harger, David Hoover, Abida Jafari, Terry Kreid, Benji Leal, Paul Lytle, Gail Michniewski, Heather Mooney, Daniel Morgan,

Hadley Mozer, Anastasia Pankau, Mary Romero, Michael Santana, and
Sandra Yowell. Finally, much thanks goes to Randy Elrod, my personal
Barnabas, and to all those other friends who have been supportive of my
written work and my lectures, who have wrestled with me through the
many issues raised by C. S. Lewis, and who have helped me to understand better the challenges of the modern and postmodern world. A full
list of these special people would take up far too much space, but I would
like to offer at least a baker's dozen of those who were most influential in
terms of this book: Mike Bellah, James Blandford, Philip Costopoulos,
Carol Drollinger, John Eidsmoe, Wade Filmore, Al Kresta, Pierre Matta,
Stan Mattson, Stanley Santire, Peter Schakel, Peggy Smith, and Dan
Stickle. A thanks, as well, to my editors, Len and Carolyn Goss, for their
unceasing encouragement and advocacy.

1

The Education
of Lewis Agonistes

Early Days:
The War of Reason and Intuition

Clive Staples Lewis was born on November 29, 1898, in Belfast, North Ireland, a city known for its wrestling between the old and the new, the medieval and the modern. Somehow Lewis and his Irish Protestant parents seem to have skirted any involvement in the issues plaguing the peace of their city, and Lewis himself, to his enduring credit, never displayed any anti-Catholic bias or animus in his writings. Still, wrestling was in the air, and the wrangling influenced Lewis in a way that is neither political nor religious. Behind the troubles between Catholic and Protestant in Ireland lies a more subtle wrestling: that between the traditional and the modern, the mythic and the mundane, the imaginative and the pragmatic. The struggle (elucidated most fully in Yeats's poem, "September 1913") is really one for the Irish soul. It is a battle for self-identity: will Ireland be a country of poets or a nation of shopkeepers?

Anyone who takes up an anthology of British literature and studies its table of contents will notice that something very strange occurs in the late nineteenth-century selections. Though the majority of poets and prose writers who appear in the premodern section of the anthology hail from England, once the anthology reaches the 1890s and then spills over into the twentieth century, nearly all the important literary authors become Irish. The list is an impressive and imposing one: George Bernard Shaw, Oscar Wilde, William Butler Yeats, James Joyce, Samuel Beckett, Dylan Thomas, Seamus Heaney, and C. S. Lewis.

The reason for this aesthetic shift from England to Ireland is not fully clear, but I would suggest that it has little to do with education or ethnicity and everything to do with soul. During the Victorian Age, England cast off much of her traditional Christian and medieval heritage and replaced it with a new faith in science, progress, and technology. This new spirit invigorated the work of such English writers as Alfred, Lord Tennyson and Matthew Arnold. However, when this faith in progress ground to a halt in the late nineteenth century, England, unable to recapture her lost biblical and medieval heritage, was left spiritually, emotionally, and aesthetically dry. Not so Ireland, which was still rich with tradition, traditions stored in her Catholic rituals, her closeness to the soil, her myths and legends, and her songs, ballads, and dances.

The young Lewis grew up with two possible identities to choose from: the reserved, modern, practical, scientific-minded English Protestant, and the passionate, medieval, sacramental, intuitive Irish Catholic. He drew on both strands and nurtured a love both for logical debate and the numinous world of faerie. He grew up in a house full of books, none of which were forbidden him, and he read deeply in a number of different styles and genres. Some of the works he loved as a child include *The Tales of Beatrix Potter, Alice in Wonderland,* the adventure stories of H. Rider Haggard, the novels of Sir Walter Scott, the Arthurian and fantasy tales of William Morris, the Sherlock Holmes stories of Sir Arthur Conan Doyle, Norse mythology, the tales of Rudyard Kipling, and romances of the Middle Ages such as *The Faerie Queene* and *Sir Gawain and the Green Knight.* In some of these works, it appears he was attracted to the fantasy; in others, he was equally attracted to the systematic structure and the wealth of concrete detail. Perhaps in an attempt to combine these two elements, the young Lewis, with the help of his beloved brother Warnie (born in 1895), created his own systematic fantasy world that the brothers dubbed "Boxen." Though populated by dressed animals and imbued with the exoticism of India, the world of Boxen is actually a very realistic, even pedestrian place with a concrete history and geography and lots of pragmatic, political adult talk.

Lewis would spend much of his life trying to reconcile the two sides of Boxen within himself, a struggle made more difficult by the fact that his parents embodied the two sides of the emotional/rational coin. As Lewis himself informs us in his spiritual autobiography, *Surprised by Joy* (1955), his parents and their families could not have been more different. Whereas his father, Albert Lewis, was a passionate, quixotic man who was easily hurt and apt to make sudden, impulsive, even illogical decisions, his mother, Florence Hamilton, was a cool, logical woman with a disciplined mind (she held a B.A. in math) and a more steady temperament. Lewis tended to gravitate toward his mother and grew up with "a certain distrust or dislike of emotions as something uncomfortable and embarrassing and even dangerous" (chapter 1). This tendency increased manyfold when his mother died of cancer in 1908, and his father, unable to handle the strain, impulsively shipped his grieving son off to a British boarding school that Lewis despised. The shock of these two events following so soon upon each other caused the nine-year-old Lewis to enshrine his mother and her cooler approach to life, and to pull away from his father and the unruly emotional life that led Albert to make such a hasty and irrational decision. Lewis's relationship with his father remained a troubled one, and the two never really reconciled, a fact that caused Lewis much guilt in his later years.

Still, Lewis's favoring of his mother's more rational temperament was balanced by three legacies of his childhood that helped to keep alive the wrestling between fantasy and practicality, intuition and logic. The first was his simple nurse, Lizzie Endicott, who filled the young Lewis's head with Irish legends and provided him with a link to the peasantry of the Irish countryside. It was from this woman, Lewis remembered, that he first learned that goodness and education, virtue and sophistication do not always go hand-in-hand.

The second legacy that nurtured in the young Lewis a love of and respect for the numinous side of life was set in motion in 1905 when the Lewis family shifted their residence to Little Lea, a large country home which they often referred to simply as the New House. It was not a particularly well-built house; its corridors were too long, and its improperly placed drains and chimneys subjected its inhabitants to endless drafts and the moans and rattling that accompanied them. All of this may have upset Alfred and Flora, but, as far as their children were concerned, it transformed the house into a fairy castle. In what is perhaps one of the most memorable sentences in *Surprised by Joy,* Lewis explains: "I am a product of long corridors, empty sunlit rooms, upstairs indoor silences, attics explored in solitude, distant noises of gurgling cisterns and pipes, and the noise of wind under the tiles" (chapter 1). In one of those upstairs rooms was an old wardrobe where Lewis and Warnie would often sit to plan out Boxen. It was a beloved piece of furniture that would one day provide Lewis with the inspiration for the magic doorway that ushers the four Pevensie children into Narnia in *The Lion, the Witch and the Wardrobe.*

Lizzie and Little Lea helped nurture in Lewis a sense of mystery and of the sacredness of the ordinary. Were it not, however, for a third legacy—a vital series of experiences that dotted Lewis's childhood—the other two legacies would not have been strong enough to champion the cause of the imagination and the supernatural that fell under increasing attack as Lewis grew more and more reliant on logic, science, and naturalism to provide him with a framework for his life. The first of these experiences occurred when Lewis was perhaps three years old. His brother, Warnie, by gathering some moss and twigs and arranging them on the lid of a biscuit tin, had just fashioned himself a makeshift toy garden. Eager to share his new creation, he brought it into the nursery and showed it to his little brother. Lewis's glimpse of that garden (and his later recollection of that glimpse) transported him to an Eden of moist and fertile greenness. "As long as I live," he would later write in *Surprised by Joy,* "my imagination of Paradise will retain something of my brother's toy garden" (chapter 1).

Lewis would have many more such experiences throughout his youth, experiences that would fill him with an intense, overwhelming desire for an indefinable "something" that was just beyond his grasp. The adult Lewis would later name this desire "joy" and would insist that, though the feeling produced by this desire was a pleasant one, the true nature of the experience was upward and outward, away both from the physical object that inspired it and the internal feelings associated with it. The experience of joy was not an end in itself, but a beacon or a signpost that pointed beyond itself to a richer, fuller, more intense world that was both supernatural and super-sensible. It offered a glimpse, an intimation of a higher mode of being that transcended the limits of earthly science and human logic. In *Surprised by Joy,* Lewis goes on to list two more such experiences. The first seized him while he was reading Beatrix Potter's *Squirrel Nutkin* and found himself strangely troubled by "the Idea of Autumn." The second came even more suddenly and unexpectedly when his eye caught hold of these words in a book: "I heard a voice that cried / Balder the beautiful / Is dead, is dead." At the time, the young Lewis knew little about Norse mythology and even less about Balder, but when he read the words, he found himself spontaneously filled with a sense of cold, remote northern regions, a sense that he would later dub "northernness" and that would inspire in him a passion for Wagner's *Ring Cycle* (chapter 5).

Indeed, one of Lewis's lifelong friendships was ignited by his discovery that he was not alone in his love for northernness. The year was 1914, and, though Lewis was home for the holidays, his brother Warnie was still away at school. To ease his boredom, the teenaged Lewis decided to visit an invalid neighbor of his named Arthur Greeves who was three years his senior. Upon entering Arthur's room, Lewis spied, lying open on a table near the invalid's bed, a book of Norse mythology. With a flash, the two boys discovered that they shared that same "stab of Joy" that came from the North (chapter 8). From that moment on, most of Lewis's closest friendships (particularly his well-known friendship with J. R. R. Tolkien, whose *Lord of the Rings* offers a perfect blending of faerie magic and systematic detail) were predicated on a mutual experience of joy.

Schooldays:
Building a Wall of Reason

Well before his sixteenth year, Lewis had already developed within himself the two competing sides of his psyche. On the one side was an eager young scholar and rationalist who yearned to hone his already sharp mind on the whetstone of reason and logic. On the other was the passionate dreamer who thrilled to the tales of Norse mythology and who sought in every nook and cranny of the world some object or story or word that would carry him away on the wings of joy to that richer world he could only catch in glimpses. As he passed through his teen years and proceeded on to college, these two competing sides, perhaps inevitably, attracted to themselves a host of opposing ideologies. Thus (as intimated above) while the rationalist gravitated toward all that was modern, scientific, and progressive, the dreamer clung to all that was medieval, religious, and traditional. For most of the first half of his life, the force of the former orientation proved much stronger than the latter. Indeed, his school years, those that stretch from the death of his mother in 1908 to his acceptance as a student at Oxford in 1917, mark a period in Lewis's life when the claims of reason seized the upper hand and almost squelched the lover of myth, romance, and mystery.

Between 1908 and 1914, Lewis attended four different boarding schools (Wynyard School, Campbell College, Cherbourg Preparatory School, and Malvern College), all of which he heartily disliked. What little faith he had in God and the efficacy of prayer had already been weakened by his unsuccessful attempts to convince God to heal his mother. To be catapulted a mere four weeks later out of his house and into a squalid school run by a sadistic and capricious headmaster (Robert Capron) who frequently beat and humiliated Lewis and his fellow classmates was more than his faith could bear. True, his experiences would drive him closer to his brother, teach him the value of friendship as he was forced to bond with his fellow sufferers against a common enemy, and lead him to long for vacation and home with a hope and a faith that he would later transfer to his spiritual yearnings for heaven. Nevertheless, these things offered small consolation at the time, and Lewis's only real defense was to try to bury himself in his books and keep his feelings and his passions locked up inside.

Fortunately for Lewis's sanity, he received some relief at Cherbourg (1911–13), where he not only received excellent instruction in Latin and Greek but found a much-needed mother substitute in the person of Miss Cowie, the gentle and loving matron of the school. Despite these high points, however, Cherbourg was the place where Lewis lost his early Christian faith, due partly to the occult interests of Miss Cowie. As the older Lewis would later realize, his fledgling interest in the occult would not mark a return to his youthful experiences of joy. Intimacy with God and a deeper appreciation of the wonders of his creation were not the spurs to his brief flirtation with spiritualism; rather, it was his desire for control without accountability, for a method that would allow him to order his chaotic world through sheer willpower that drove the young introvert toward the mysteries of the occult. At Cherbourg, Lewis also found another way of taking control; it was here that he first learned to be a fop and a snob (due partly to the influence of a young schoolmaster whom Lewis nicknamed "Pogo"). In *Surprised by Joy,* Lewis recalls that Pogo first taught him "the desire for glitter, swagger, distinction, the desire to be in the know" (chapter 4). By donning the mask of a modern, fashionable man about town, Lewis could shield himself both from the indignities associated with British boarding schools and from his own unfulfilled yearnings for joy. But the mask would soon crack.

If Cherbourg introduced Lewis to the bright side of snobbery, then Malvern opened his eyes to the dark side. For it was here that he first met the "Bloods," the upper-class athletes who formed the aristocratic elite of the school and who ruled over underclassmen like Lewis with absolute power. Younger boys were expected to be at the continual beck and call of the Bloods, ready to carry out, without complaint, any menial task assigned to them. This system, known as fagging, was accepted by most students as one of the rules of the game. Just as American college students who wish to pledge a fraternity gladly put up with the ritual humiliations of "hell week" since they know it will win them a coveted place on the "inside" where they will eventually earn the privilege to impose their own "hell week" on next year's pledges, so the typical British schoolboy put up with the fagging system without much complaint. Indeed, many of them, including Warnie, throve under it and considered it one of the processes that "made them a man." Not so the sensitive, nonathletic Lewis. He hated intensely the self-importance of the Bloods and the time-wasting duties they imposed on him, and he devotes much space in *Surprised by Joy* to condemning the fagging system. Indeed, throughout his adult life he considered as one of the great evils the human desire to be part of an "inner ring." For Lewis this desire provoked a double evil in the soul, for those people on the inside pridefully considered themselves above the human herd, while others on the outside would resort to the basest fawning and toadying in order to secure their own spot on the inside.

Lewis would have nothing to do with "Bloodery"; rather, he would fashion his own intellectual system unsullied by the yearnings for acceptance that drove his fellow underclassmen to abase themselves before the athletic elite. Eventually (and inevitably) he would fall under the sway of the materialistic psychology of Sigmund Freud and would, for awhile, dismiss his own yearnings for the supernatural as merely a species of wish fulfillment. Everything, both inside and outside, would be subjected to ruthless analysis, introspection, and demystification. He would build a new and stronger wall to shield himself from the Bloods, from his father, and from his own deeper desires. And to guide him in building that wall, he would turn to a master builder: William T. Kirkpatrick.

Though Albert Lewis had for many years ignored or misunderstood his son's continual pleas to be rescued from boarding school, in 1914 he finally conceded to Lewis's request and sent him to a private tutor whose main task it would be to prepare Lewis to take the entrance exams that would secure him admission to Oxford. Known to the Lewis family variously as Kirk or "the Great Knock," Kirkpatrick, who had been Albert's tutor many years earlier, lived in Great Bookham in Surrey, England. From listening to his father's sentimental recollections of the Great Knock, Lewis had expected to encounter a kindly old man who would hug him and tell him funny stories; nothing could have been farther from the truth. From the very moment Lewis arrived at Great Bookham, Kirk beat into his head the need for clear, rational thinking that was free from all subjective speculation and emotional murkiness. Their very first meeting set the tone for the two years of instruction that would follow.

The young Lewis hated small talk and avoided social gatherings as often as he could. However, as he believed that all adults favored such small talk as a necessary component of polite conversation, he decided to greet his father's beloved Kirk with a choice bit of meaningless chitchat. And so, after firmly shaking his new tutor's hand, the nervous Lewis suggested to Kirkpatrick that Surrey was less "wild" than he (Lewis) had expected it to be. Lewis had spoken well, but his attempt at adult conversation fell on deaf ears. Kirkpatrick hated small talk even more than Lewis did. Rather than answer back with an equally innocuous comment on the weather, Kirk subjected Lewis to an immediate, deadly serious inquisition as to the basis of his statement. The inquisition did not last long; it quickly became apparent to Lewis that, as his expectations of Surrey were wholly unfounded (and ungrounded), and as he did not even know what he meant by the word *wild*, that his statement was both illogical and meaningless and had best be dropped. Most students would have crumbled under such relentless logic; to Lewis it was "red beef and strong beer" (chapter 9). From this point on, he committed himself to absolute clarity of thought and to identifying and assessing the assumptions on which our ideas and our beliefs are based.

Kirkpatrick, a member of that venerable old school of Scotch empiricists who trace their lineage back to David Hume, was both a skeptic and an atheist. Lewis, at this time in his life, was also an atheist, and under Kirkpatrick's tutelage, he learned the art of debunking all thought that was based on emotion or intuition or faith. He learned, too, that through logic and reason he could build a wall of self-protection that would shield him from all in life that was vulgar, chaotic, and irreducible. He could free himself from the wrestling, from the uncertainty that had plagued his childhood.

But his rational house of cards was just about to begin its slow tumble.

Oxford:
Breaking Down the Wall

Despite the growing shift toward a modern rationalistic-naturalistic mind-set that marked his teenage years, Lewis continued, even while suffering under the Bloods at Malvern or studying under the Great Knock at Surrey, to experience moments of Joy. The experience could be initiated by almost anything: a landscape, a few lines of poetry, the sound of ducks flying overhead, even a phrase. His love for Norse mythology continued unabated as well, as did his fascination with Wagner and all things northern. The imaginative richness of his early childhood was still there all around him, but Lewis was at grave risk of losing his ability to access it.

As though at war with his own spiritual longings, Lewis would again and again kill the experience of joy by focusing on the feeling it produced rather than using that feeling as a springboard to jump towards higher truths. Worse yet, rather than let the thrill come naturally and spontaneously, he would seek to reproduce it and hold on to it through manipulation of his own emotional states and excessive introspection. One moment embracing an antimystical materialism, he would dismiss the joy as an illusionary wish fulfillment; the next moment embracing an antirational occultism, he would convert the joy into a ravenous, pseudo-erotic lust for dark secrets and forbidden wisdom. He wanted the joy and wanted it desperately, but he refused to surrender to it, refused to let go and embrace the mystery. He was willing to perhaps accept a spiritual force behind the world, but he was by no means willing to accept a personal God who was the source of all his yearnings and who desired his obedience, his will, and his love.

Then one day in 1916, while returning home by train from Surrey on holiday, Lewis purchased an inexpensive little book that started within him a mental, emotional, and spiritual revolution. The book was titled *Phantastes: A Faerie Romance,* and its author was George MacDonald, a Scottish minister born in 1824, whose passionate, if at times somewhat heterodox, love of Christ found various expression in unspoken sermons, moral tales, children's stories, and works of high fantasy.

Phantastes, first published in 1858, is one of the strangest and most unpredictable books in the language. Virtually plotless, it tells the adventures of Anodos, an ordinary, even mundane character who, while ruffling through his father's writing desk, comes upon a fairy who ushers him into an enchanted world where all of nature, from the tallest tree to the tiniest flower, is alive and where magical doorways and passages abound. After spending only a few hours in this mysterious world of faerie, Anodos is nearly killed by a wicked ash tree, but then is saved by a gentle beech who gives him a garland of flowers to protect him. Sometime later, Anodos comes upon a beautiful lady encased in marble. He sings her awake and then follows her as she runs off into a cave. Once inside the cave, the lady (who is an alder tree in disguise) seduces him and steals his beech leaves. Again, the ash attacks, only to be defeated by the blow of an axe wielded by Sir Percival, a wandering knight who has himself been seduced by the wicked alder. From here, the adventures of Anodos get (to quote that nineteenth-century visitor to another magical land) "curiouser and curiouser." In one episode, he enters the house of an ogre, and uncovers, in a hidden closet, his own shadow, a dark, relentless *doppelganger* that pursues him throughout the novel. In another episode, he comes upon a palace that contains a magic library with the power to allow its reader to enter directly into the world of books. In yet other episodes, he witnesses a goblin dance; enters a cottage with four doors that lead to the past, to sighs, to dismay, and to the timeless; and assists two sibling princes in slaying three dragons, a deed that wins him the status of hero and leads him to accept the role of squire to Sir Percival. In the final episode, Anodos, after being killed by a wolf, feels his soul leave the physical restraints of his body and become one with all of nature.

The book is a strange one, even to the modern reader accustomed to fantasy, and the reading of it had a profound impact on the seventeen-year-old would-be naturalist. As he turned the last page of the book, Lewis realized that something mystical, something almost inexplicable had happened within him: his imagination had been baptized (*Surprised by Joy,* chapter 11). For the first time, he sensed the power of holiness and caught a glimpse of a higher spiritual level toward which his early experiences of joy had been pointing him. Reading the book did not make him a Christian (that was still many years away), but it did perform two vital tasks. First, it allowed him to perceive, even in the most mundane of objects, a supernatural light beaconing from a fresher, more emphatic world. Second, it helped drive him toward a vital realization about his experiences of joy: the fact that he continually desired something that the natural world could not supply suggested that another, supernatural one existed that was the origin of that desire. The desire did not, of course, guarantee that he would achieve that other world, but it did suggest to Lewis that he was a creature who was capable of achieving it and who was in some sense made to achieve it.

In time, this realization would develop into one of Lewis's most powerful apologetics, generally referred to as the argument by desire. For the young Irishman, it opened up the shocking possibility that his experiences of joy had a real origin and promised a real destination. Orthodox Christianity (and even theism) were still far off, but the experience of reading *Phantastes* had opened the door a crack and ushered in a beam of light that would, in time, grow brighter than the sun. Lewis would later claim that he did not recall writing a single book where he did not quote MacDonald in some way; indeed, when the time came for Lewis to write his own mini-version of Dante's *Divine Comedy* (*The Great Divorce*) he would choose MacDonald to be his Virgil-like guide through heaven.

Lewis's encounter with *Phantastes* occurred near the end of his tutelage under Kirkpatrick and prepared him well for the next stage in his spiritual and intellectual education: Oxford. His years as a student at University College, Oxford stretched from 1917 to 1923 (with a brief hiatus in 1918 during which he fought and was wounded in World War I) and were followed by another thirty years during which Lewis taught in various capacities at his beloved Magdalen College. (From 1954 to his death in 1963, Lewis served as the Chair of Medieval and Renaissance Literature at Magdalene College, Cambridge—same name, different spelling—however, even while teaching at Cambridge, he continued to spend his weekends and holidays at his home in Oxford.) Lewis eventually became something of a fixture at Oxford, but his early years there were ones of intense personal struggle during which the wrestling between reason and intuition, modern and medieval reached its height. Lewis Agonistes was about to throw himself fully into the ring, and his antagonists were to come in the form of both books and friends.

In the years that followed his reading of *Phantastes,* Lewis slowly and reluctantly came to the realization that whereas all the writers he most respected and was most challenged by (Dante, Spenser, John Donne, George Herbert, Milton, Samuel Johnson, G. K. Chesterton) were all Christians whose beliefs played a central role in their writing, all those authors whom he considered somewhat pretentious, thin, and hollow (Voltaire, Gibbon, John Stuart Mill, Bernard Shaw, H. G. Wells, D. H. Lawrence) were all opposed, in some way, to traditional Christian beliefs. Only in the poetry and prose of Christian writers did Lewis catch any glimpses of that sacred holiness he had experienced in *Phantastes* and in his own encounters with joy. Indeed, even in his reading of classical Greek and Roman authors, it was always those authors with the fullest religious sense (Plato, Aeschylus, Virgil) who spoke to him most powerfully. "A young man who wishes to remain a sound Atheist," wrote Lewis in *Surprised by Joy,* "cannot be too careful of his reading" (chapter 12).

But it was the people he met and worked with as a student and professor that truly challenged his preconceptions about Christianity. When his contemporary, Owen Barfield, began his studies at Oxford, he was, like Lewis, an atheist. But then, to Lewis's great shock and surprise, Barfield started embracing a supernatural understanding of the world and, horror of horrors, even began to look back to the medieval period as a positive era in European history in which humanity was closer to nature and possessed a more direct, unmediated wisdom that rested not on empiricism, logic, and reason, but on imagination, inspiration, and intuition. From Barfield, Lewis encountered the phrase "chronological snobbery," an affliction which Lewis soon discovered that he himself suffered from. Chronological snobbery, as Lewis defines it in *Surprised by Joy,* is "the uncritical acceptance of the intellectual climate common to our own age and the assumption that whatever has gone out of date is on that account discredited" (chapter 13). All ages, of course, possess some degree of this temporal arrogance, but the modern age was perhaps most enslaved to it because of its near worship of progress, positivism, and technological improvement.

For all his scholarly discipline and all his wide reading, Lewis had failed to engage directly the assumptions of his own age. Before meeting and wrestling with Barfield (via a long philosophical debate that they dubbed the "Great War"), Lewis had simply taken for granted that if the majority of thinkers around him asserted that medieval ideals and Christian virtues were outdated and illogical, then surely some great logician must have long ago disproved those "archaic" notions and shown them to be faulty. Of course, once Lewis was challenged to explore this unconscious assumption, he quickly discovered that no such "logician" had ever existed. Even more disturbing, he began to meet real, live, flesh-and-blood colleagues who still believed very passionately in these archaic notions and felt no cognitive dissonance in holding to them while simultaneously living and working in a modern university. Of all these colleagues, perhaps the one that most deflated Lewis's long-held (if finally baseless) prejudice against the values of medieval Christendom was Nevill Coghill, a professor still remembered today for his fine verse translation of *Canterbury Tales* into modern English. In Coghill, Lewis encountered a man who actually lived by the standards of medieval courtesy and chivalry, whom Lewis could almost imagine fighting a duel. And yet, despite the fact that he embodied a way of life and a method of thinking and believing that Lewis had previously thought primitive if not barbarous, Coghill was (by Lewis's own admission) "the most intelligent and best informed man" in his class (chapter 14). The young atheist, it seemed, need not only be careful of his reading, but of his friends as well.

However, of all the friends that Lewis met at Oxford, the one who had perhaps the most profound impact on his journey toward Christianity was J. R. R. Tolkien, a committed Catholic and professor of Anglo-Saxon who, though six years his senior, proved a perfect soul mate for Lewis. Indeed, in addition to their shared faith, the two men would fight side by side to preserve at Oxford the traditional English curriculum that placed a heavy emphasis on medieval language and literature and to raise worldwide the sagging reputation of such "archaic" genres as romance, allegory, and fairy stories. What first drew the two together was their mutual love of Norse mythology, and Tolkien helped reignite Lewis's love of all things northern by inviting him to join the Coalbiters, a society founded by Tolkien for the purpose of reading aloud the *Sagas* and the *Eddas* in their original Old Norse. As they read and discussed the legends of the Norsemen, and as Lewis felt his old passions stir again, Tolkien gently inspired him not only to take myth seriously as a vehicle of truth and beauty but to explore more fully and carefully the links between myth and Christianity.

Though Lewis's final conversion was predicated in part on a slow process of rational "self-apologetics" that helped open his mind to the possibility that God existed, a truth he accepted in 1929, reason and logic alone would never have brought him before the person of the Incarnate Christ. The key to his final embrace of Christian doctrine (as opposed to mere theism) was, in fact, his love of myth and his childhood experiences of joy, which had already been strengthened by his reading of *Phantastes*. Still, despite the fact that his delight in myth and accompanying yearnings were very real to him, until he met Tolkien, Lewis was prevented from being led to Christ by these yearnings because he stubbornly insisted on interpreting the meaning of myths through a modernist framework. As a disciple of *The Golden Bough* (1922) of Sir James Frazer, he accepted without question its underlying assumption: namely, that the Gospels, with their dramatic reenactment of a divinely born hero who rises out of obscurity, performs miraculous healings, suffers a sacrificial death, and then triumphantly returns in a glorious resurrection, merely mark another telling (albeit a more sophisticated one) of an ancient myth that is repeated again and again throughout the ancient world. Taking a premise similar to the later writings of Joseph Campbell, Frazer had argued (and Lewis, like a dutiful modern, had agreed) that myths, whether pagan or Christian, possessed archetypal power and spiritual significance, but had no historical or "rational" value. A myth could make you feel good, inspire you, or help you understand elements of your psyche, but it certainly wasn't "real" in any sense that it could serve as the basis of truth claims or demand any kind of accountability.

So Lewis thought until, in the fall term of 1931, he and Tolkien (along with another Christian colleague, Hugo Dyson) took an all-night walk around the grounds of Magdalen. As they walked, they engaged in a free-for-all discussion during which Tolkien suggested to Lewis a different way of interpreting the mythic elements in the gospel accounts of Christ. Perhaps, he submitted, Christ seems mythic to us because he is, in fact, the myth made true. Perhaps if Christianity seems mythic it is because all the great myths of the ancient world have found their literal and historic fulfillment in the birth, death, and resurrection of Jesus Christ. This simple suggestion, one that is explored in the closing section of Tolkien's seminal study, *On Fairy-Stories,* opened the floodgates and allowed Lewis to combine into a single stream his rational, twentieth-century brain and his intuitive, myth-loving heart. Within two weeks, he would confess himself a full believer in Christ.

But to make that confession, one last element would have to fall into place. "Lewis Agonistes" would not become a true wrestler until he learned to take seriously the full implications behind the spiritual truths with which he had been sparring. This biographical account stated earlier that Lewis devoted much of his teen years to building around himself a self-protective wall of logic and rationality. His motivation for building that wall was not purely intellectual; much of it came down to his personal dislike of being interfered with. Lewis was essentially a private person who just wanted to be left alone to read his books and think his thoughts, free from any interference by an outside force. True, he spent much time meditating on religion and questioning the existence of God, but he had no desire to meet that God face-to-face. Spiritualism was for him a method for seizing control of the unseen powers around him, not for surrendering his will to a divine Creator. He was, to use one of his own metaphors (*Miracles,* chapter 11), like a boy playing cops and robbers in the attic. Anyone who watched such a boy at make-believe would think that he would be thrilled to encounter a real robber, but, of course, were that same boy to hear the sound of footsteps coming up the stairs, he would quickly end his game and run for cover.

When Lewis, the supposed seeker of spiritual truth, heard the divine footsteps on the stair, he was no more anxious than the boy in the attic to confront the reality. Indeed, by his own admission, Lewis was a miserable and unwilling convert, dragged kicking and screaming into the kingdom of God as he vainly cast his eyes in every direction seeking a means of escape (*Surprised by Joy*, chapter 14). For the first time, the awesome nature of human choice and the eternal consequences that follow what we choose loomed before the self-protective reader of books and thinker of thoughts. Lewis's milieu was a deterministic one that tended to downplay human volition in favor of larger, impersonal structures. But now, it seemed, Lewis would have to make a decision, or, better, surrender to a certainty larger than himself and the petty structures of modernist ideology. He would learn then the truths that he would later share with his readers—that the Trinity, the claims of Christ, and the miracles that undergird Scripture were realities that both he and his age had to deal with. They could no longer be ignored or dismissed as mere myth. They had to be wrestled with, and Lewis Agonistes would be the man dubbed to take up the challenge.

Christian Apologist: The Marriage of Reason and Intuition

In order to make the transition from theist to Christian, Lewis had, in many ways, to put aside the rational logician and become instead the intuitive lover of myths. Luckily, however, he did not stop here, but moved forward to effect a fusion of these two sides of his character. Thus, when in 1931 he followed the joy-trail to its final end and surrendered himself to the piercing love of Christ, he did not simply jettison his early mental training for an emotional, pietistic faith. He was still the disciple of the rational Kirkpatrick, and when the time came for him to write his great apologetical works—*The Problem of Pain* (1940), *Miracles* (1947), *Mere Christianity* (1952)—he would marshal the full force of his logical mind in defense of the central doctrines of the Apostles' Creed. Unlike so many of his contemporary Christian academics who passively (if not unconsciously) accepted the existing assumptions on which their disciplines were based and then meekly asked that God's name be mentioned now and then, Lewis went on the offensive and challenged the assumptions themselves. He would not allow Christian faith to be marginalized as a personal belief or private affair; he would drag the whole Christian framework—doctrines, values, miracles, and all—back into the public, academic agon. He would defend the intellectual status both of the ancient creeds and the medieval worldview, and he would demonstrate that, though the would-be Christian must finally come to a point where he must take a step of faith, that step need not be an irrational, existential leap into the void.

However, had Lewis brought to Christian apologetics only his skills as a logician, his works would not, I believe, have been as effective as they were (and still are). The mature Lewis tempered his logic with a love for beauty, wonder, and magic. His conversion to Christ not only freed his mind from the bonds of a narrow stoicism; it freed his heart to embrace fully his earlier passion for mythology. During his rational years, Lewis had felt the need to submerge his youthful love for fairy stories; his newfound faith in a God-Man who died and rose again reopened for him the enchanted world of his childhood. Apart from this dash of fairy dust, Lewis might have become yet another dry, systematic thinker (an Aristotle, Aquinas, or Calvin); instead, he speaks to us with all the power and life-changing force of a Plato, a Dante, and a Bunyan. Nearly all of Lewis's insights into the Christian faith can be traced back to a comment made by one of the Church Fathers or one of the Medieval Scholastics, but then these commentaries are seldom read (except by specialists), while Lewis's works continue to sell, challenge, and convict in the millions.

Lewis was and is unique, for he understood both the heart that yearns for God and the mind that seeks to know him. Just as Plato's greatest dialogues (*Republic, Phaedo, Phaedrus, Symposium*) begin with a logical defense of, say, the immortality of the soul, and then end with a myth in which that rather stale doctrine leaps into vital life, so Lewis was never content merely to prove the existence of God or defend the necessity of a key Christian doctrine. Yes, Lewis will provide us with the scholastic proof, and he will do so in what Wordsworth called "the real language of men," but he will not let us rest until we acknowledge and feel the overwhelming reality and presence of that God whom Lewis describes, variously, as the hunter, the lover, and the bridegroom.

Thus, while he continued to write his "rational" works of apologetics, Lewis also devoted his energies to embodying the truths and values of traditional Christianity in two series of fictional works and one myth-based novel. In the first of the series, the space trilogy (composed of three novels written between 1938 and 1945, *Out of the Silent Planet, Perelandra, That Hideous Strength*), Lewis would use the genre of science fiction to encourage his readers to rethink the tenets of medieval cosmology and chivalry and to understand the dual nature of reality (physical/spiritual) in a refreshing new way. In his beloved seven-part Chronicles of Narnia (1950–1956), Lewis, revivifying the often patronized genre of children's literature, would create an entire mythical world where both the theology and the choice-laden ethical framework of Christianity would spring into thrilling life. In 1956, he would follow up these series by writing a single, complex novel (*Till We Have Faces*) through which he would incarnate Tolkien's argument that the myths of the pagan world point toward the historical coming of Jesus Christ.

But Lewis would not stop there. Between his rational apologetics and his imaginative fiction, Lewis would carve out a middle ground where the radical creativity of his Chronicles could blend with the argumentative power of *Mere Christianity.* He attempted to find his voice first in the years immediately following his conversion by retelling his journey to faith in the form of a spiritual allegory that he titled (after Bunyan) *The Pilgrim's Regress* (1933). This first attempt proved a bit too arcane for most readers, though it embodies Lewis's faith that if we follow out our experiences of joy to their final end, they will lead us to Christ. Nevertheless, Lewis remained undaunted and followed *The Pilgrim's Regress* with two works that are among his greatest and most enduring accomplishments: *The Screwtape Letters* (1942) and *The Great Divorce* (1946). In the former, Lewis provides us with a series of letters in which a senior devil attempts to instruct his nephew in the fine art of temptation. In the latter, Lewis allows us to take a fabulous bus ride from hell to heaven and to eavesdrop as the souls of the blessed attempt (mostly unsuccessfully) to convince their damned friends and relatives to put aside their sin and accept the grace of Christ. In both works, Lewis succeeds in telling a cracking good story while instructing his readers in the eternal nature of our choices. Indeed, Lewis was so enamored of the epistolary form of *The Screwtape Letters,* that near the end of his life he chose to embody some of his views on prayer, sacrament, and the Christian life in a series of fictional letters (that one can hardly believe *are* fictional) that he called *Letters to Malcolm,* published posthumously in 1964.

Although Lewis's conversion released something within him that led him to write over thirty books in as many years, his surrender to Christ also marked the virtual end of Lewis's endeavors in two other literary areas. In the years preceding 1931, Lewis had consistently and conscientiously kept a journal of his thoughts and struggles. When he became a Christian, however, he immediately put down his journal and never took it up again. Likewise, in his pre-1931 years, Lewis had great aspirations to be a poet and actually published two (unsuccessful) volumes of poetry, *Spirits in Bondage* in 1919 and *Dymer* in 1925. Though Lewis would now and then compose a poem, the shift to prose he began with *The Pilgrim's Regress* would quickly become an almost total one. Indeed, as a sort of farewell gesture to Lewis the poet, he incorporated much of his early poetry into the pages of *The Pilgrim's Regress.* Why, the biographer of Lewis must ask, did Lewis choose to leave his journals and poems behind when he entered into the second, Christian phase of his life? Lewis certainly did not consider either of these genres to be negative or un-Christian (indeed, the great Christian poets of the past had played a central role in his conversion). Nevertheless, he seemed to feel, in his own case at least, the need to abandon his early private-poetic endeavors in favor of a more direct, external prose. The inner struggle would have to transform itself into a public wrestling.

Lewis would come to feel that both he himself and his post-Freudian age were too introspective. True, as a lover of Plato, Lewis would continue to believe in and advocate for the necessity of self-knowledge; but he would make a vital distinction between the true spiritual, emotional, and intellectual growth that rises up out of a fuller understanding of one's fallen nature and potential in Christ, and the self-centered solipsism that results from an incessant self-analysis that would explain one's origin, choices, and purpose solely on the basis of unconscious, material, deterministic forces. To put it simply, Lewis stopped thinking about himself and moved the dialogue out onto a public stage where ideas really mattered and where the consequences of those ideas, for good or for evil, were not only of perennial interest but were both timely and urgent. Indeed, in recognition of Lewis's ability to speak on the contemporary value of traditional beliefs in a public, non-esoteric way, the War Department asked him to perform a rather unique service for his country. During the dark days of World War II, when London was being attacked from the air by an often invisible enemy, Lewis was invited to deliver over the radio a series of Broadcast Talks (1941–1944) on the ethical and theological teachings of the Christian church that were later collected and edited into book form under the title, *Mere Christianity.* After Churchill, Lewis's voice became one of the most recognized on the British airways, and everyone from the research scientist to the poor soldier in the pub tuned in to hear this once timid Oxford professor of English expound the basic tenets of the Christian faith in a robust, straightforward prose style of great power and lucidity.

Lewis's conversion, with its concomitant fusion of the two strands of reason and intuition, freed him as an apologist to speak a more direct and universal language; it also freed him as a professor from that over-specialization that had been seizing the halls of academe since the Enlightenment and the Industrial Revolution. The modern scientific mind, Lewis would come to argue, tended toward an almost mechanical division of labor that called for an assembly line of narrowly educated specialists who lacked a wider vision. Lewis, in the tradition of the great medieval and renaissance thinkers that he loved, would fashion himself rather into a generalist whose all-encompassing imagination would seek a fuller conception of man, God, and the universe. Lewis *would* write many specialized works—most notably, *The Allegory of Love* (1936), *A Preface to Paradise Lost* (1942), *English Literature in the Sixteenth Century, Excluding Drama* (1954), and *The Discarded Image* (1964)—but all of these books would be informed by a wealth of reading in numerous genres and a broader understanding of worldviews and how those worldviews interact with what people think, feel, and believe. Indeed, in one of his most important and prophetic books, *The Abolition of Man* (1943), Lewis would explore carefully the negative and possibly dangerous impact of modern educational methods and theories that embrace a relativistic, values-free ideology.

If we were to judge Lewis's postconversion years solely on the basis of the above paragraphs, we might conclude that Lewis became a full-time writer who spent most of his waking hours locked up in a study with a typewriter before him. Nothing could be further from the truth. He continued his wrestling not only on the printed page but before several generations of students. His university lectures, attendance at which was voluntary for Oxford students, always gathered large crowds and were famous for their clarity and their depth and breadth of coverage. Lewis had a gift for diving into a veritable sea of primary material and coming up with a handful of aesthetic pearls. For those students who desired to understand the worldview that informed such epic works as Dante's *Divine Comedy,* Spenser's *Faerie Queene,* and Milton's *Paradise Lost* but did not have the desire or patience to sift through the pedantry, Lewis proved an invaluable resource as well as an entertaining and humane guide.

Outside the classroom, Lewis also participated actively in two groups at Oxford that allowed him to keep both sides of his psyche—the rational and the imaginative—well oiled and in active shape. The first of these was called the Oxford Socratic Club, a group which was founded by a student (Stella Aldwinckle) but which boasted Lewis as its President from 1942 to 1954. The purpose of the group was to allow an open forum for the discussion of the relevance and intellectual soundness of supernatural Christianity in a modernist, naturalistic world. The ideal meeting would consist of two opposing papers on the same general topic (for example, miracles or materialism or dogma) read by a Christian and an atheist; if no willing atheist could be found to speak openly before the Club (a not uncommon problem) the two papers would be read by Christians who held opposing views. After the papers were read, the floor would be thrown open for discussion. Anyone could speak, but what everybody waited to hear was Lewis's refutation of the atheist. Lewis was happy to oblige. It was at such meetings that Lewis honed his apologetical skills and helped raise the intellectual status of Christianity within the academic world.

The second group, which Lewis himself founded with the help of Tolkien in 1933, was the Inklings, an informal club that allowed its members the chance to read aloud their fictional and nonfictional works in progress. Though nearly all the members, including Warnie, Coghill, Barfield, Dyson, Charles Williams, and, eventually, Tolkien's son and editor, Christopher, were committed Christians, and though the conversation naturally gravitated toward spiritual issues, the focus of the group was not theological but literary. It was at such meetings, for example, that Tolkien first read drafts of his now-famous *Lord of the Rings* and where Lewis first delighted an audience with the breathtakingly beautiful landscapes of *Perelandra*. The formal meeting of the Inklings occurred weekly on Thursday nights in Lewis's apartments in Magdalen College, Oxford; however, so enthusiastic were its members that they also met, more informally, at a local pub on Tuesday mornings. All the members, especially Lewis and Tolkien, benefited greatly from the critiques of their work and from the sense of fellowship and camaraderie. Though not all the members wrote in the genres of fantasy, science fiction, and children's literature, they were all eager to see these genres revived and encouraged Lewis and Tolkien in their seminal endeavors in these fields.

By allowing his gifts for rational argument and logical precision to combine with his rich imagination and with his own spiritual yearnings for joy, Lewis matured into the greatest apologist of the twentieth century and one of the most adept wrestlers in the modernist arena. In the thirty-two years that followed his conversion (which, significantly, fell almost exactly in the midpoint of his earthly existence), Lewis both reinvented and reinvigorated the content, method, and purpose of apologetics. While excelling in what must always remain the central focus of apologetics—the logical defense of the core doctrines of Christianity—Lewis expanded the field to include at least four other areas: 1) the uncovering and defining of competing worldviews and of the assumptions that underlie those worldviews; 2) the marshalling of fiction, mythology, and other "nonrational" genres in the struggle against a materialistic modernism that would exclude the supernatural; 3) the positioning of Christianity as the end point and fulfillment of all the highest and deepest yearnings of the human species; and 4) the blending of a reformed Protestant focus on salvation by grace through faith with a more medieval Catholic focus on the freedom of the will and the eternal consequences of our daily choices.

In all these areas, Lewis would wage his agon, and it is no exaggeration to say that every Christian apologist since Lewis has been influenced by his wrestling in one way or another. However, before throwing down the towel and retiring from the ring, Lewis was to wage a final battle in his own personal life that would mold and shape him in ways he could never have predicted or imagined.

The Last Battle: Wrestling with Love and Pain

While fighting in the trenches of World War I, Lewis had befriended a fellow soldier named Paddy Moore. In one of those youthful moments of optimism and devotion, the two young men took a vow that if either of them perished in the war, the other would take over the care of the dead man's family. As fate would have it, Paddy was killed in 1918, and shortly thereafter, Mrs. Janie Moore (along with her daughter Maureen) moved in with Lewis, an arrangement that continued until Mrs. Moore's death. Between 1919 and 1925 (when he finally received a full-time position at Oxford), Lewis was dreadfully short of cash; yet, throughout his long years of poverty, he continued to provide a home for Mrs. Moore and her daughter. Lewis's almost superhuman devotion to Mrs. Moore was grounded, of course, on his promise to Paddy, but there was certainly more to it than that. Lewis clearly loved Mrs. Moore as a surrogate mother; indeed, his love for her was so strong that many have suggested the two had a sexual relationship. Whatever the extent of their relationship, Albert and Warren clearly disapproved of Lewis's close ties to Mrs. Moore and were quite bewildered at the extent of his devotion. Many eyewitnesses were horrified at how Lewis was continually at the beck and call of Mrs. Moore; at the slightest word from her, he would drop what he was doing and run out to any store to buy any requested item. Still, it is clear that in some respects Mrs. Moore gave more than she took, providing Lewis with much needed domestic stability and preventing him from becoming too absorbed in his books. Mrs. Moore helped to draw Lewis out and taught him to be the genial host he would become famous for; it was she who arranged to shelter WWII children in his Oxford home, the Kilns, an experience that prepared Lewis to write his Chronicles of Narnia. In matter of fact, without Mrs. Moore there would have been no Kilns, since she put up most of the money to purchase it. In her later years, Mrs. Moore tended to become quite bossy and irascible (some of the vignettes of petty domestic tyranny that enliven and enrich the pages of *The Screwtape Letters* and *The Great Divorce* are certainly based in part on Lewis's experience of the manipulative side of Mrs. Moore), but Lewis never ceased in his devotion to her.

Perhaps because of his devotion to Mrs. Moore, Lewis, like Warnie, remained a bachelor and saw no need to complicate his already busy life with thoughts of matrimony. However, when Mrs. Moore died in 1951, the domestic side of Lewis—and for all his protestations of "bachelordom," there *was* a domestic side to him—was freed for a shift of direction. Indeed, almost immediately after her death, Lewis began to foster a close friendship with the woman who would become his future wife, Joy Davidman.

As unlikely as it may seem, the future Mrs. Lewis was a divorced, nonpracticing Jew from the Bronx who spent many years as a self-avowed atheist and communist and who was not averse to vulgar language and antisocial behavior. Joy's first husband, William Gresham, was, like Joy herself, a writer of some merit—movie buffs will be interested to know that Gresham wrote the novel on which the 1947 Tyrone Power film *Nightmare Alley* was based. Both Joy and Bill eventually converted to Christianity, partly through reading the apologetical works of Lewis, but Bill, an alcoholic like the character in his novel, fell away from his newfound faith and proved to be chronically unfaithful to his wife.

Lewis had first "met" Joy in the year before Mrs. Moore's death via an exchange of letters. Despite his hectic schedule, Lewis always took the time to answer letters from his numerous fans (the majority of them women), a time-consuming process that led him to compose enough letters to more than fill four five-hundred-page, single-spaced volumes. The practice caused much pain to his already rheumatic hand, but it allowed him to carry his wrestling on to the most personal of arenas and kept him in touch with the spiritual needs and desires of ordinary people. With some of his fans, Lewis corresponded frequently; Joy was one such fan. Indeed, when Lewis finally met her face-to-face in 1952, he felt that he already knew her. He would soon get the chance to know her even better.

In 1953, the newly divorced Joy took her two sons, David and Douglas, and moved (she hoped permanently) to England, where she would often visit the Kilns and spend long hours in conversation with Lewis. Unfortunately, two years later, Joy learned that her visa was about to expire and that she would have to return to America. She appealed to Lewis for help, and he, never one to let down a friend, agreed to marry Joy in a civil ceremony in order to secure her British citizenship. At this point, love and romance were the farthest things from Lewis's mind; for all he knew, he would live and die a bachelor. But his affections for Joy had grown more powerful than he had expected. When he learned a year later that Joy was dying of cancer, his latent love for her rose to the surface, and he arranged to marry her in an ecclesiastical service held at her hospital bedside.

The doctors did not expect Joy to survive more than a few weeks, but then, miraculously, her cancer went into remission. She was soon strong enough to move into the Kilns, and she and Lewis began a three-year honeymoon that Lewis considered the happiest years of his life. Joy proved the perfect soul mate for Lewis, and she not only inspired him to write *Reflections on the Psalms* and *The Four Loves* (two works that pushed Lewis into yet other untapped regions of the field of apologetics), but served as the model for Lewis's most fully realized fictional character, Orual, the heroine of *Till We Have Faces*. Due to her often abrasive personality—not to mention her status as a divorcee—many of Lewis's friends disapproved of the marriage, but Lewis's devotion to her was unwavering. By his own admission, he was being allowed by God to experience in his fifties the kind of happiness usually reserved for people in their twenties. The fact that his wife's name was Joy only increased

Lewis's sense that she was a person who could also fill some of his earliest and most long-standing yearnings.

Unfortunately, the honeymoon was a brief one; Joy's cancer soon returned, and she died at home in July of 1960, just three months after taking a tour of Greece with Lewis and their friends. Though her death was expected, the loss of Joy devastated Lewis and sent him into a deep depression. As a way of handling his grief, Lewis began to keep a diary of his spiritual and intellectual struggles. He soon discovered that he had filled four journals, and, though he had not originally planned to publish his musings, he quickly realized that what he had written might prove useful to other people suffering the pain of loss. Eventually, the journal entries were published (at first anonymously) under the title of *A Grief Observed* (1961). The book is a brief but profound work that has come to be recognized by many as one of the greatest studies of grief ever written (to my mind, only Tennyson's *In Memoriam* surpasses it). What makes the work so unique and memorable is that Lewis is brutally honest. He did not, as many Christian writers would have done, go back and edit the early notebook entries so as to make them seem less despairing or more orthodox. Far from a simple inspirational book, *A Grief Observed* is an authentic journal of a deep, almost existential despair which slowly resolves itself into a refound faith. It is the work of a mature Christian who has seen much and experienced much, and it carries the cool logic of Lewis's earlier study of suffering, *The Problem of Pain,* onto a higher realm of wisdom where resolution comes through intense struggle and where neat, tidy answers give way to an almost mystical surrender to truths that are too wonderful for mortal men to know.

Lewis's own death would follow but a few years hence, and the Lord would reunite him with Joy (and his experiences of joy) on that same fateful day, November 22, 1963, when John F. Kennedy fell prey to an assassin's bullet. It was a day that marked a coming of age experience for millions of naïve and sheltered citizens across the United States, who would be forced to rethink their beliefs and preconceptions about the nature of the world and the fallen men and women who live in it. It would be a difficult battle and a long one, but it would be an agon that had already been carried on by a self-protective atheist turned triumphant Christian wrestler who well deserves to bear the title of "Lewis Agonistes."

2

Wrestling
with Science

Unpacking the Modernist Paradigm

Ever since the Scopes Monkey Trial of 1925, American Christians have been engaged in an ongoing debate over the origin of the earth and the various species that live on it. At times the debate has centered on whether the "days" described in Genesis 1 are literal twenty-four-hour days or represent eras of indefinite length. At others, the issue is whether God created the earth directly as a potter shapes an urn or worked "behind the scenes" through the natural processes of evolution. At yet others, the focus is shifted to asking the more general question of whether or not the world bears testimony to the creative hand of an intelligent designer. What few realize, however, is that lurking behind the surface of this multifaceted argument lies a greater, more far-reaching debate: one that lies at the very heart of the distinction between traditional and modern. Indeed, the wider issue, of which the evolution-creation debate is but a subcategory, is one that, if pursued down to its roots, will enable us to unearth what I shall call the modernist paradigm.

Before the nineteenth century, most Europeans possessed a world-view shaped by a theology grounded in the Bible and a philosophy that traced its roots back to Plato. Central to both of these traditions was a belief that the nature of reality was top to bottom. That is to say, the real, the essential, the original resided above in a spiritual heaven, while all that lay below in this physical, natural world was created by, descended from, or was an imitation of those original heavenly presences. The spiritual was the primary; the physical was the secondary. Though the central Christian tradition often found itself at odds with the Platonic over the final status of the physical (with the former affirming the intrinsic value and "salvageability" of the flesh, and the latter tending to dismiss it as a prison and even an illusion), both agreed that the ultimate origin of the imperfect, ever-changing, time-enslaved flesh was something perfect, unchanging, eternal, and spiritual.

For Plato, this top-down paradigm found its fullest expression in his theory of the Forms: the belief that everything in our perishable, bodily World of Becoming is an imitation of an imperishable Form (or Idea) that exists in a nonbodily World of Being. Thus, although our world contains a vast array of different types of chairs, all of these chairs point back to (because they descended from) a single, perfect Chair which resides above in the heavens and which embodies the eternal essence of "chair-ness." In the same way, our earthly grasp of such abstract nouns as beauty, truth, justice, and goodness can all be traced back to an Absolute Beauty, Truth, Justice, and Goodness that dwell in unchanging perfection in the World of Being. Whereas Greek mythology taught that the origin of the world and even of the gods themselves was an amorphous but physical "cosmic soup" that they called Chaos, and whereas such sixth-century B.C., Pre-Socratic philosophers as Thales and Anaximander attempted to posit a single, physical substance (water, air, etc.) as the arch-substance out of which life arose, Plato moved philosophy toward a metaphysical framework that privileged and gave primacy to that which is unseen and noncorporeal.

Still, although Plato points Western philosophy in that direction, it is really only in the biblical, Judeo-Christian tradition that we encounter the clearly stated belief that a divine, eternal being created the universe *ex nihilo* (out of nothing). By using this Latin phrase, Christian theologians and philosophers asserted that in the beginning there was God and only God; physical matter is not coeternal with God but was created *by* him. Reality begins with God and finds its ultimate and purposeful origin in him alone. So is it for the universe; so is it for we humans and for all those aspects of ourselves and our culture that we hold most sacred. Language, laws, ethics, religion, truth, beauty: all were seen as finally divine creations whose origin was from above but whose original purity was tainted by contact with our fallen world. The principle that ruled both natural and human life on this earth was not evolution but entropy, not progress but decay. The role of the theologian was to interpret, not invent, divine revelation; the role of the scientist was to rip away the veil and uncover the handiwork of God spread throughout the cosmos. Both were to think God's thoughts after him. Both also worked within a top-down hierarchical framework (known as the Great Chain of Being) in which glory and essence stretched downward from God through the various orders of angels to man, and then continued, in a carefully calibrated spiral, down the multitudinous ranks of animals, plants, and minerals.

So the majority of Europeans viewed their world and their relationship to its Creator for almost two millennia. But then, beginning slowly and sporadically in the eighteenth century and accelerating and widening in the nineteenth, the traditional paradigm on which Western metaphysics had long rested began to shift. Perhaps the Great Chain was not a golden thread let down from heaven by a personal, spiritual being, but an impersonal, mechanistic staircase built from the ground up. Perhaps the nature of reality was not top to bottom but bottom to top. With the help of new scientific methods, humans would slowly begin to seek their origins from a different direction: one that was physical rather than spiritual, impersonal rather than personal. After two thousand years of looking upward for answers, the shapers of Western culture would turn their eyes downward. Mother Nature would replace God the Father as our parent and as the ultimate source not only of the universe and of humanity but of all those elements that most define us as a species. The paradigm had shifted, and it would have repercussions in every area of human thought, from science to religion, from anthropology to economics, from philosophy to psychology, from classical philology to biblical hermeneutics.

—⚉—

In high school and college textbooks that trace the growth and development of Western intellectual history, four names tend to compete for the honorary title of Father of Modernism: Darwin, Freud, Marx, and Nietzsche. All, of course, are worthy candidates, but what is often left unstated is that all four of these thinkers shared fully in the same modernist paradigm and helped to extend it into their respective fields of study.

Perhaps the most vital and irreplaceable of the four is Darwin, for his theory of the evolution of species through natural selection was the glue that enabled modernism to hold together as a respectable alternative to traditional Western thought. Any intellectual paradigm must be able to answer, at least in schematic form, how the human species came into being, and, to be quite frank, until Darwin came along, no believable option to biblical creation really existed. Yes, several of the Pre-Socratic philosophers (most notably Thales, Anaxagoras, Empedocles, and Democritus) toyed with early "rough drafts" of the modern theory of evolution. Their ideas even reached literary form in Lucretius's first-century B.C. Latin epic, *On the Nature of Things,* but few people outside their tight-knit circles took their theories seriously. First Plato and Aristotle, and then the Doctors of the Church discredited their theories, and it was not until the nineteenth century that a real attempt was made to revive a naturalistic explanation for the origin of the human species.

Let me repeat myself. Without this naturalistic explanation, the modernist paradigm could not have flourished as it has. The fact of the matter is that we are here, and there are really only two options for how we got here: either we were created and put here by a higher being or we evolved into our human state through natural, physical processes. The third possibility, that we were put here by an alien race, is not really an alternative; it merely tables the creation/evolution debate and reconvenes it at a far earlier time and a far distant place. If Europe was to adopt a new bottom to top paradigm, she would first need to reassure advocates of that paradigm that our own existence could be explained fully through impersonal, wholly material forces. Darwin provided this reassurance, and, by so doing, provided also the founding myth upon which all of modernism rests. Be ye not deceived: the creation account in Genesis 1 and the theory of evolution are *both* myths, inasmuch as they are etiological stories that can neither be proven nor repeated but on which our understanding of our world and our place in that world rests. The traditionalist need not be surprised that the modernist clings to his theory of evolution with the same stubborn tenacity as the fundamentalist Christian clings to his belief in a literal, six-day creation. Evolution both defines and enables the entire approach and direction of modernist thought; it is the one thing that can neither be compromised nor sacrificed.

Darwin, then, is a founder of modernism, for he carried the bottom to top paradigm into the realm of the biological sciences. He outlined a counter-system to traditional entropy, one in which things progress from the physical to the spiritual, the less complex to the more complex, the material to the immaterial. But he was not the only nineteenth-century thinker to construct such a counter-system.

Just as Darwin was putting the finishing touches on his theory that the human body could have evolved from lower animal forms, Sigmund Freud was just beginning to explore how the conscious human mind could also be defined and shown to have developed by natural processes alone. For Freud, our *psyche* (Greek for both mind and soul) is not a divine gift that descended from above but a material product of dark, unconscious, impersonal forces. In traditional metaphysical thought, our limited, personal self-consciousness is but a reflection of that greater, unlimited self-consciousness that rests in the mind of God (that God whose name is, simply, I AM). For Freud, who turns the traditional paradigm on its head, the origin of our self-conscious thoughts and desires is not to be sought in a *supra*-conscious being (top to bottom) but in a complex web of *sub*-conscious patterns (bottom to top). As Darwin pictured human bodily life as the end point in a fierce animal struggle for survival, so Freud pictured the human psyche as the end product of another kind of animal struggle waged well beneath the surface of conscious thought. Indeed, far from posting the spiritual as the origin of the psyche, Freud would argue that our highest spiritual thoughts are merely illusory wish fulfillments whose source is physical. What the Bible calls love (*agape* in Greek; *caritas* in Latin) is not, for the modernist Freud, a human reflection of a divine Form proceeding out of a Being who *is* Love; rather, it is a sublimation of a baser, material desire for food and procreation. Freud was a materialist, not because he sought to accumulate wealth—the more recent sense of the word—but because, in keeping with its philosophical definition, he only believed in the existence of matter. The spiritual was not only *not* the origin of the physical; it did not even exist.

Karl Marx, the third founder of modernism, shared fully Freud's materialistic worldview, a view that, though it is not essential to the modernist paradigm, is fully compatible with it and represents its final and logical end point. What Freud did for psychology and Darwin did for biology, Marx did for that multidisciplinary field in which history, sociology, political science, and economics all meet. In keeping with the modernist bottom to top orientation, Marx argued that human political and cultural systems did not flow downward out of the mind of God or even out of the thoughts of a visionary set of Founding Fathers, but evolved upward out of deep, material structures and dumb, impersonal forces. Marx identified these forces with the economic means and modes of production, and he posited that they formed a substructure on which all social, political, religious, and aesthetic thought rested. As both citizens and human beings we are products of this substructure. To put it another way, we do not create our economic system; our economic system creates us.

A century later, French historian Michel Foucault would develop Marx's modernist paradigm further to show how not only the things we say and believe, but even the thoughts we think are products of a vast web of power that rises up from below rather than descending from above. Literary theorists, too, would jump on the modernist bandwagon and argue that great poets like Shakespeare, far from transcending the time and place in which they lived and wrote, were themselves products of that time and place. Building on the theories of both Freud and Marx, many in the academic community today reject the traditional notion that great poetry descends downward via inspiration from God to the poet to the audience. Both the poetry and the very consciousness of the poet are to be understood as having "evolved" out of social-political-economic forces that are not only beyond the poet's control but of which the poet is generally ignorant.

The fourth Father of Modernism is Nietzsche, yet another material-ist whose great contribution to the modernist paradigm was his debunk-ing of truth. When Nietzsche declared that God is dead, he meant not only to deny the existence of God but of any and all absolutes that would claim a separate, unchanging existence apart from man and the products of man's labor. What we call "truth," Nietzsche argued, is not some eter-nal verity descended from above, but something that man himself thought up and then forgot that he thought it. Picture an ancient Greek sculptor who carves an idol of Athena and then hides it behind a bush. Twenty years later, he returns to the same bush, "discovers" the idol, and declares triumphantly that the goddess Athena has sent her likeness to earth as a divine gift. What he has forgotten, of course, is that he himself was the creator and origin of the idol. Once again, the direction of cre-ation, of truth, of reality is revealed to be not top to bottom but bottom to top.

In this basic assumption, Darwin, Freud, Marx, and Nietzsche all agree. Indeed, they and their modernist heirs would remain so commit-ted to this basic down-up orientation that they would bolster it with a shift in the main method by which they acquired the knowledge on which they built their theories. I speak here of a general shift from deductive to inductive logic that also took hold in the nineteenth cen-tury. For those whose acquaintance with formal logic is rusty, induction is a kind of reasoning that begins with observed facts and figures and then proceeds upward toward a more abstract hypothesis or inference. A doctor who takes a patient's symptoms and then, on the basis of this empirically collected data, arrives at a diagnosis, is making use of induc-tion. So, too, a jury that gathers evidence and then declares a verdict on the basis of that evidence is participating in a kind of inductive reasoning. Deduction, on the other hand, begins with abstract premises and general assumptions and works its way downward toward a specific conclusion. Christian (and Platonic) thought is deductive, for it begins with *a priori* assumptions that must be accepted as givens before logical thought can begin (e.g., the existence of God, the authority of Scripture, the immortality of the soul, and the possibility and reliability of divine revelation). A traditional moralist accepts first the primacy and integrity of the Ten Commandments revealed by God to Moses, and then applies those commandments to a specific ethical situation. A traditional scientist or astronomer takes for granted that the laws of nature and of the cosmos are perfect and balanced, believing also that the God who created them is himself perfect and balanced. From this standpoint, one can then go on with confidence to uncover and catalogue those laws.

Generally speaking, modernism has rejected the deductive, up-down method of research as a faulty, subjective, even tautological way of arriving at truth. In contrast the modern practitioners of induction claim that *their* conclusions are based solely on empirical observation and are therefore objective, unrestrained by any prior assumptions or presuppositions.

—∞—

Such are the methods and presuppositions that undergird the modernist paradigm and link together the theories and writings of Darwin, Freud, Marx, and Nietzsche. But the influence of modernism has proven to reach far wider; its octopus-like tentacles have stretched out to embrace disciplines well outside the circle of those from within which the four founders did their pathbreaking work.

Anthropology, for example, has swallowed whole the modernist notion that culture and religion evolve from the bottom up, from less complex to more complex, primitive to civilized. Thus, whereas the traditional, biblical account asserts that we all began as monotheists but then fell away into polytheism, pantheism, idolatry, and animism, modern cultural anthropologists since Sir James Frazer (see chapter 1 for his influence on the young C. S. Lewis) have argued exactly the opposite. Belief in a single God does not precede animism but rises slowly out of an evolutionary process that develops upward from animism to pantheism to polytheism to monotheism. (It might be added here that most anthropologists would continue to extend that development past monotheism into what they consider the highest form of knowledge and certainty—science.) Modern linguists, as well, reject the traditional notion that language was a perfect, divine creation that subsequently (as a result of human sin and pride) devolved into a multitude of less exact languages. In direct contrast to what we might call the Tower of Babel thesis, the last century of linguistic studies has put forward a "flip-flop" thesis in which primitive, simplistic languages branch out and evolve into higher-order languages. The fact that, at least grammatically speaking, modern languages are simpler than those spoken by the ancients seems not to bother these upholders of the modernist paradigm.

One would expect that theologians and biblical scholars might at least offer a critique of this paradigm, but, alas, they, too, have bought into the modernist worldview (though they at least have not combined it with the materialism of Freud and Marx). Until the modern period, Jews and Christians alike accepted almost without question the Mosaic authorship of the Torah or Pentateuch. But the evolutionary mind-set initiated by Darwin and his fellow founders quickly cast doubt on this long-held faith. A prolific and "scientific" school of biblical critics known as "higher criticism" sprang up in the late eighteenth century and eagerly applied the new modernist methods to their study of the Pentateuch. Their conclusion, dubbed the "documentary hypothesis," was that the Pentateuch was not the creation of a single mind (Moses) divinely inspired by a greater Mind (God) but was the product of a long process of textual evolution. They identified four distinct phases of this evolutionary process and marked each of those phases with a different, descriptive letter (J, E, P, and D). During each phase, and even between the phases, a series of editors with different agendas, perspectives, and theologies continued to edit and reedit the slowly evolving text. To them the evidence was clear. Moses did not write the Torah; the Torah "wrote" Moses.

Meanwhile, in the world of New Testament criticism, the letters and theology of St. Paul were subjected to the same modernist, evolutionary treatment. Rejecting the traditional notion that Pauline theology was primarily a gift of divine revelation (albeit filtered through the social and ecclesiastical crises of the first-century church), modernist scholars asserted that his theology evolved over a period of two hundred years (which is to say, of course, that Paul could not have written all of his epistles). Those letters whose theology, Christology, soteriology, and eschatology seemed primitive and "early" were ascribed to Paul, while those letters with "ologies" more sophisticated were left to unnamed second-century authors. The Gospel of John, too (with its advanced Christology), was left to be constructed by second-century authors. The problem was not just that a poor fisherman like John could not be expected to have written such a refined work; *no one* in the first-century church could possibly have propounded a doctrine so complex and "late." Remember, according to the bottom to top direction of modernism, theology does not descend downward from divine revelation, but evolves upward from more physical changes in church politics, leadership, and ideology. The fight over Moses and Paul still rages today, but the traditional date of the fourth Gospel was, almost miraculously, confirmed and restored by a scrap of papyrus containing verses from the eighteenth chapter that conclusively dated the Gospel to no later than the 90s A.D. That vital scrap (which single-handedly demolished an entire school of German higher criticism) is known as the Rylands Papyrus; it offers clear proof that God has a sense of humor.

Classical philologists, not to be left off the modernist bandwagon, focused their attention on those other two books that, like the Old and New Testament, have both founded and shaped Western culture and belief, the *Iliad* and *Odyssey*. At the same time that the biblical critics were debunking Moses, the classicists set about debunking Homer. The *Iliad* and *Odyssey* were no longer to be seen as the creation of a single, conscious mind that drew together and shaped the oral tradition into a work of aesthetic beauty; Homer was to be reduced to just one of many bards in a long, finally impersonal process of editing and reediting, addition and revision. Just as Moses was to be considered a creation of the

Pentateuch, so the *Iliad* and *Odyssey* were to be given credit for creating Homer, and not vice versa. Indeed, unashamed to make the link between the debunking of Moses and Homer, Gilbert Murray, in his seminal work *The Rise of the Epic,* illustrates his evolutionary view of the authorship of the *Iliad* and *Odyssey* by offering a capsule overview of the documentary hypothesis! Let us not be confused on one vital point—traditional scholars of Genesis and the *Iliad* were well aware of the influence of oral tradition on Moses and Homer; they simply accepted that this oral tradition was collected under divine, or at least poetic, inspiration by Moses and Homer and shaped by them into the works that bear their authorship. What was unique about nineteenth-century studies was not the discussion of the oral tradition but of the way higher criticism reinterpreted the role of that tradition through a paradigm grounded in evolutionary thought.

Finally, the bottom to top orientation of modernism has even found its way into a philosophical school that has exerted much influence on European thought: existentialism. The well-known existentialist motto, existence precedes essence, embodies perfectly the modernist paradigm. Human nature, choice, and destiny, this three-word mantra asserts, do not proceed out of some prenatal essence called a soul that was shaped by a divine and personal being. They are, rather, man-made concepts fashioned by creatures who are not in fact creatures, but fatherless blank slates who must invent their own essences and purposes as they go along. There is no divine calling, no preexistent spirit, no "up there," just a purely physical, uncaring world run by natural processes into which we are born naked and unprepared.

The Things That Could Not Have Evolved

The above paragraphs should suffice to open the reader's eyes to a way of thinking that has become so diffuse, so universal that it is almost invisible. Indeed, few thinkers ever state the paradigm itself; they just take it for granted and pursue their studies accordingly. That all human phenomena can be defined and explained as the end product of natural, impersonal, mechanistic forces is, for the vast majority of Americans and Europeans, not to mention the citizens of other countries that have been bitten by the modernist bug, a given that need never be questioned or doubted.

Until his conversion in 1931, C. S. Lewis also accepted without question the modernist paradigm. But after that life-altering event that transformed Lewis in heart, mind, and soul, he began slowly to question and doubt the evolutionary presuppositions upon which all of his previous knowledge had rested. Indeed, again and again in his major apologetical works, Lewis confronts his readers with a series of human phenomena that could *not* have evolved—that is to say, that could not have arisen from natural, material causes alone. At present, there are many Christian scholars and writers who have uncovered flaws in Darwinian evolution (most notably, Philip Johnson and Michael Behe) and have cast doubt on the ability of time plus chance to create such complex structures as cells, especially via a system of slow, incremental change. Their work has been greatly helpful and often refreshingly pointed, but by focusing so much of their attention on the natural sciences they have left untapped more humanistic areas that touch people at a much deeper and more familiar level.

When Lewis Agonistes took on the modernist paradigm, he chose to do so in an arena of everyday experience: one in which ordinary men and women, if they could only develop eyes to see and ears to hear, would be enabled to witness all around them the necessity for divine, supranatural origins. And the place he started was in that special arena that was most familiar and personal to him—his childhood experiences of joy.

We have already discussed how Lewis, from a very early age, was visited by almost mystical moments in which a mundane object or event (the toy garden made by his brother; Beatrix Potter's *Squirrel Nutkin*; a few poetic lines on the death of Balder) suddenly opened before him a window onto a fresher, more intense world. It was an experience that Lewis would come to learn was essentially universal. Have we not all experienced sudden moments of suspension during which our souls and minds are lifted up by a yearning for something other, something rich and strange, something (and this is the vital part) that our natural, merely human world cannot supply? What can possibly be the source of this yearning, this moment of joy? It certainly cannot be something from our own world since the very nature of the desire points the one experiencing it beyond the limits of the physical and the earthly. The desire must itself flow from a reality that transcends the physical, one that can act as a legitimate source and origin.

All this carries us to what is perhaps Lewis's most original contribution to apologetics, the argument by desire. In the first chapter of this book, I offered a schematic definition of this argument; I shall now offer a fuller one informed by the modernist paradigm which it is meant directly to challenge. The argument runs thus: Just as the fact that we experience thirst is proof that we are creatures for whom the drinking of water is natural, so the fact that we desire an object that our natural world cannot supply suggests the existence of another, supernatural one. The desire does not guarantee that we will achieve that other world (if stranded in the desert, we will die of thirst), but it does suggest that we are creatures who are capable of achieving it and who were in some sense made to achieve it. Those who would explain all by the process of evolution fail to explain why and how that process would evolve in us a yearning for realities that lie outside that very process and that cannot be satisfied by it. True, the bottom to top paradigm can account for our yearnings for food, sex, and shelter, but the chasm that separates these natural urges from the experience of joy is one that is not quantitative but qualitative. In other words, while our natural urges may be refined bit by bit quantitatively so as to produce in us a desire for more tasty food, a more beautiful mate, even a more expensive home, the leap that takes us from these still earth-centered desires to a yearning that would leave all that is earthly behind is one that is essentially and qualitatively different. The one cannot evolve into the other; one might as well claim that because a tennis ball and an orange share the same shape and color that the latter developed out of the former.

In the final chapter of his *Reflections on the Psalms,* Lewis extends and reformulates his argument by desire in such a way as to offer a stunning and original defense of the immortality of the soul. Did you ever note, he asks his reader, how odd it is that we are continually surprised by the passage of time? We see a younger acquaintance we have not seen for ten years and are shocked to see how tall the child has grown; we celebrate our twenty-fifth anniversary and reflect back on how impossible it is that the years could have rushed by so quickly. Though most people think nothing of this phenomenon, Lewis steps back and considers it from a removed vantage point. Surely this common human behavior is a strange one. Given the fact that time is the element in which we live, that we have, in fact, known nothing but the incessant succession of past, present, and future since we breathed our first breath, it is decidedly odd that we should be so consistently shocked at its passage. Indeed, our surprise at the passage of time would be tantamount to a fish being continually surprised by the wetness of water. "And that," Lewis concludes, "would be strange indeed; unless of course the fish were destined to become, one day, a land animal." Both our constant surprise at the passage of time and our yearnings for something our world cannot supply suggest strongly that we were made for a reality and a mode of being that transcends both time and space. (It should be noted here that the Freudians *do* have a pat answer for the argument by desire, but I shall save that answer, and Lewis's critique of it, for the conclusion of this chapter.)

In many ways, Lewis's joy apologetic marks an updating and an expansion of a single line from Augustine's *Confessions*: "Our hearts are restless, Lord, until they rest in thee." As a Christian who learned to integrate within himself the rational and the intuitive, Lewis would not allow the logical side of apologetics to obscure what is perhaps the strongest argument for God's existence: our unquenchable need and desire *for* him.

Modern apologists, most of whom have cut their eye teeth on Lewis's works, would say that we all have a God-shaped vacuum in our hearts that only Christ can fill. We try vainly to fill that void ourselves with all manner of earthly things, some good and some bad, but nothing can heal the eternal ache save the Being who placed it there. Lewis makes this very argument in the final chapter of *The Problem of Pain*: "Your soul has a curious shape because it is a hollow made to fit a particular swelling in the infinite contours of the divine substance, or a key to unlock one of the doors in the house with many mansions." What we truly need, what we truly lack, cannot be supplied by the physical, impersonal "stuff" out of which the modernist paradigm would have us evolve. We must turn our eyes back upward again if we are to find an origin and a source capable both of creating that lack and fulfilling that need.

—⁓—

Such is Lewis's emotional, intuitive argument as to why not everything in our world is susceptible to a material, mechanistic explanation of cause and effect. He was to offer others, ones that did not rely on feelings and personal experiences but were grounded in a bracing logic that would force even his Scotch empiricist tutor, Kirkpatrick, to stand up and take notice. Whereas his argument by desire is worked out most fully in his two personal literary autobiographies (*Surprised by Joy, The Pilgrim's Regress*), his more logical grapplings with the modernist paradigm surface in his three standard apologetical works: *Mere Christianity, The Problem of Pain,* and *Miracles.*

Lewis begins his finest and best known work of apologetics, *Mere Christianity,* by noting something rather odd: when two people disagree over an issue of right and wrong, they solve their disagreement, not by fighting, but by arguing. The very fact that they argue rather than fight suggests that they have tacitly agreed to a common standard of ethics and morality. If they did *not* accept this common standard, their argument would be futile, and they could only solve their differences by sheer, brute force. A father and mother do not argue over whether or not good parents are those who care about their children. They both accept that as a given (an *a priori*), and then each attempts to prove (deductively rather than inductively) that his or her approach toward child-rearing best approximates their shared standard. If they did not agree on this standard, there would be no basis for their argument.

But of course they *do* agree, just as all sane people agree that murder and lying and stealing are wrong. That is not to say that people guilty of murder, deceit, or theft will not defend their actions, but they will generally do so within the parameters of an accepted ethical standard. They will argue, for example, that the killings they committed were not really acts of murder but forms of self-defense, or that their lies were really something else—exaggerations or lapses of memory. Alternatively, they may justify their thefts in the name of an even higher shared ethical standard (the necessity, say, to provide food for one's children or to promote justice and an equitable distribution of resources). But the fact remains that they accept the ethical standard as a law higher than themselves, as one not merely dictated by society but as possessing universal, even divine force. If they did not accept this standard, if they argued that the crimes they committed were, in fact, moral ones with no need of justification, they would most likely be diagnosed as sociopaths and confined to an institution.

Modern anthropologists would have us believe that there are no absolute ethical standards that are true for all human cultures. Indeed, they have been so successful in convincing us of this "fact" that most now take for granted that morality is relative and that it shifts radically from culture to culture. This is most emphatically untrue. The seemingly upside-down morality of obscure tribes that anthropologists take such glee in discovering and reporting are, in most cases, sheer invention. This is not to say that the anthropologist is consciously seeking to deceive. Rather, it is to suggest two things: 1) that those who travel great distances to find something will generally find it, and 2) that most aboriginal peoples (who possess the same capacity for making logical inferences, even if they have not studied logic) will quickly discern what it is the gift-giving anthropologist wants to hear and will be happy to oblige. But there is something even more significant at play here. Just as there are, scattered throughout the human race, mentally disturbed psychopaths who, by some genetic fluke, lack the ability for rational and ethical discernment, so there are bound to be, scattered among the various people groups of the world, a few tribes who lack the rudiments of human ethics. No one in his right mind would define normal human behavior on the basis of a handful of schizophrenics (though one *could* argue that this is exactly what Freud did!). And yet, for close to a century now, relativists who are steeped in a modernist paradigm that says that ethics are a product of impersonal evolution, rather than a gift of divine revelation have consistently pointed to the supposed amoral sexuality of various tribes in Papua, New Guinea as proof positive that the sexual standards of biblical Judaism and Christianity are merely the products of a repressed and reactionary culture.

In opposition to this entrenched assumption that morality is relative, Lewis argues in book 1 of *Mere Christianity* that universal standards *do* in fact exist and that the vast majority of people whose consciences have not been impaired by disease or self-destructive behavior recognize these standards and feel an obligation to follow them. That does not, of course, mean that they will necessarily obey these laws. Unlike the fixed laws of nature, the ethical laws of human nature always rest on a "should," an "ought," a choice of whether or not to conform oneself to the standard. Unethical and immoral behavior abounds both in individuals and in groups, but the fact that we continue to be horrified by such behavior and to condemn it as barbaric or even antihuman is merely further proof that we are all aware of the higher standards that human beings *should* conform to. Lewis further argues that these various standards are all pieces of a universal law code that transcends time and space and applies to all cultures and religions. In the first chapter of *The Abolition of Man,* Lewis dubs this law code "the Tao," and, in an appendix to that work, he essentially proves the universality of the Tao by lining up the law codes of a number of ancient cultures: Greek, Roman, Babylonian, Chinese, Hebrew, Norse, and Egyptian, among others. The amazing correspondence that Lewis uncovers in these various codes may at first shock us, given the wide array of lawgivers who gave expression to them. But the shock quickly dissipates when we realize with Lewis's help that the true role of prophets and teachers is *not* to make up the Tao but to *remind* us of those moral laws that we already know. No true teacher—not even Jesus—claims to invent the Tao; the teacher merely illustrates or reinterprets or fulfills it in such a way as to make its nature and its appeal both fresh and pragmatic. Those who *do* attempt to make up a wholly other ethical standard—whether Hitler, Pol Pot, Haile Selassie, or those terrorist leaders of our new millennium—are eventually exposed as frauds, lunatics, and/or false prophets.

Indeed, as a further and correlative proof of the universality of the Tao and of the moral force it exerts on all people, Lewis in both

Mere Christianity and *The Abolition of Man* points to the ironic fact that even people who disclaim the existence of the Tao will demonstrate in their own lives its reality and integrity. Thus, even those modernists who consider themselves complete relativists and who deny (with Nietzsche) any absolute standards of right and wrong, will be incensed if someone cuts in front of them in line. Why should they get angry, unless they have tacitly taken for granted that standards of decency *do* exist and exert a claim on all people? Many relativists will, with one breath, deny the universal validity of any moral or ethical standards, and then in the next, argue and defend passionately their belief that democratic ethics are superior to Nazi ethics. But of course, if there is no Tao, then there is nothing to say that Nazi ethics may not be superior to democratic ones.

To approach this from a different direction, many anthropologists would claim that what Lewis calls the Tao is actually just another name for a natural instinct (such as self-preservation, procreation, or protection of one's family) that has been bred in us by natural selection. Lewis writes in *Mere Christianity,* book 1, chapter 2, that at first this argument sounds like a good one, but it quickly runs into trouble. What happens when we encounter a situation in which two natural instincts come into conflict—when we must choose, say, whether to save our own lives or the lives of our family? How do we resolve this dilemma? We do it, of course, by appealing to a third thing (*tertium quid* in Latin) that will act as a standard or touchstone against which we can measure the two competing instincts. But this *tertium quid* cannot merely be another instinct, or it could not provide the removed standard necessary. The ruler that we use to judge which raw piece of wood is the right size for the fence cannot be itself merely another piece of wood. In the absence of the Tao, we are left unable to make those moral decisions that define us as an ethical species distinct from the conscienceless lower animals.

The Tao and the way it functions in our lives and our societies is an essential, irremovable aspect of our humanity, and yet it cannot be accounted for by evolutionary processes that are wholly material and impersonal. The modernist paradigm can neither explain nor account for it. Survival of the fittest might conceivably create a world in which might is always right, in which the will of the stronger defines the rules of the moment. But it cannot be the source of an ethical code that transcends time and culture and that provides a *tertium quid* against which human beings can measure their base, animal instincts. It could explain Hitler, but not our Tao-based reaction against the moral standards of his party. Nature, mired as she is in a fixed spatio-temporal field, cannot achieve the necessary removed perspective from which to fashion a universal code; only a supernatural being who lies outside of nature could create a code that operates within nature while yet remaining apart from it.

In chapter 3 of *Miracles,* Lewis extends this line of argumentation into the field of naturalistic science. Like the materialist, the naturalist argues that nature is all there is, that there exists no super-nature, no spirit distinct and apart from the physical universe. Of course, the flaw in naturalism is that it leaves itself open to the same attack as the modernist paradigm. If anything in our experience can be found that cannot be shown to have been the product of a bottom to top evolution (such as ethics and our experience of joy), then the paradigm crumbles; just so, if anything can be found that is independent of nature, that is not a part of what Lewis calls "the whole show," then naturalism is refuted. In the case of naturalism, Lewis finds this independent, super-natural element in the very laws and principles of naturalism—hence his famous, if controversial, claim that naturalism is self-refuting.

The laws of naturalism rest on abstract principles that lie outside the supposedly closed, total system of nature. To even begin to formulate such principles we must, via the power of our human reason, rise outside the flow of nature to achieve a higher perspective. Indeed, by the exercise of our human reason, we can even discover ways to alter nature. True, naturalism can allow for the amassing of empirical data and even for the drawing of simple cause and effect relationships: If I shake the tree, an apple will fall, and I will satisfy my hunger; the sun has risen every day of my life, so I can trust that it will continue to do so. But once we move from correlations to the theory of relativity or the laws of thermodynamics, we are engaging in a leap that is qualitative rather than quantitative. Once we start saying this must be this way or that ought to be that way, then we are engaging in a higher order of reasoning that nature and her physical processes know nothing about. If nature is an interlocking mechanism, then our knowledge and understanding of that mechanism cannot simply be a part of it.

Interestingly, once Lewis identifies human reason as a thing that could not have evolved, he goes on in chapter 4 of *Miracles* to effect a full reversal of the modernist paradigm. Not only could reason not have evolved from the bottom up; it must have descended from the top down. Although human reason is a separate entity unique from nature, it does (oddly) cease to operate for eight hours a day, and can even be impaired by such substances as alcohol and drugs. What, then, allows reason to continue to exist as an extra-natural substance when it is asleep? Lewis's answer is that it could only do so if it were linked in some way to a greater reason, an eternal self-consciousness that neither sleeps nor changes, in whom there is "no shadow of turning." His answer suggests that only the traditional paradigm, with its assertion that our lesser "I am" flowed originally out of a greater I AM, can offer a plausible answer to the awesome riddle of human consciousness.

—⁂—

For Lewis then, there are at least three things, joy, ethics, and human reason, that could not have evolved. In the introductory chapter to *The Problem of Pain,* Lewis adds a fourth—religion.

For quite a while now, sociologists and anthropologists steeped in the modernist paradigm have simply assumed that the origin of religion in primitive man was a fear of the unknown that evolved upward out of the less developed fears and anxieties of the lower animals. Lewis concedes that a sense of fear lies at the core of religious experience, but then makes a vital distinction between two separate kinds of fear. If someone were to tell you that in the room next to you there was a tiger, you would be afraid. In the same way, if you were told that in the next room there was a ghost, you would also be afraid. But the two fears you experienced (though masquerading under the same name) would be radically different. The first fear rests on a threat of physical danger; the second on an inner sense of awe and wonder that Lewis calls "the uncanny" or "the numinous." Yes, we experience fear, but not in the same way that we fear a wild animal, for the ghost, after all, cannot hurt us in any physical sense.

To refer again to an earlier formula, the difference between the fear of physical danger and the fear of the numinous is not quantitative but qualitative. The latter could not have evolved out of the former. The uncanny is a distinctly human thing that bears no precedent in the animal world. Though both men and animals can be frightened by other beasts, only men dread the skeletons of their own kind. Though Tarzan may shudder with terror as he trespasses upon the graveyard of the elephants, the "religion-free" pachyderm on which he rides does not share his discomfort as it treads on the ivory-rich remains of its deceased kin. Only humans fear the uncanny, and it is on the basis of this numinous fear of the unknown that religion develops. But if the uncanny could not have evolved upward from material processes and impersonal forces, then its origin must rest in some higher, nonphysical reality. Our experience of the numinous, like our experiences of joy and our inner awareness of the universal and binding nature of the Tao, drives us upward toward religion and God; yet, those very things that drive us upward would not possess the capacity and power to do so had they not been themselves gifts of divine revelation, no matter how dim and how tentative.

But Lewis's analysis of religion does not stop here. Lewis extends his argument further to take in not only the origin of religion itself but of more advanced, monotheistic religions like Judaism, Christianity, and Islam. Such religions, Lewis argues, do not come into being until that supernatural qualitative leap that made us aware of the numinous is followed by a second leap that links that numinous to the Tao. True monotheism does not exist until a connection or marriage is made between the numinous Presence who lives atop Sinai and causes the mountain to rumble, and the divine Director of the Tao who reveals to Moses the Ten Commandments. Most today simply take for granted that God, if he is truly God, must be both powerful and good, both mysterious and moral. But that is because the connection has already been made and has become an integral part of religion in the West.

Indeed, there is no natural reason why the two should be united thus, and so again we are dealing with a qualitative leap. History abounds with examples of both nonmoral religion and nonreligious morality. An example of the former would be the pagan religions of ancient Greece and Rome, religions that featured immoral gods and accepted ritual prostitution as an integral part of their sacred ceremonies. An example of the latter would be Buddhism, a religion that, though highly ethical, is atheistic in its purest form. Kali worshipers included human sacrifice as part of their devotion to the gods, while the Epicurean Lucretius advocated a strict moral code despite the fact that he believed the soul was material and would dissipate after death. But the way of the marriage of the numinous and the Tao is the more difficult (and, as such, less natural) way. It is so easy to be a Pantheist, to encounter God in every tree and hill while feeling no sense of moral responsibility or accountability in his presence. It is equally easy to muse about duty and the higher good while resting smugly secure in the knowledge that if you shirk that duty the universe won't care. But the God who reveals himself in the Bible and in Christ is an eternal yet personal Being who demands both our worship and our righteous obedience, a living God, not to be trifled with, who loves, pursues, commands, and reigns.

It's Your *God Who's Too Small*

Thus far, we have allowed Lewis to wrestle with the modernist paradigm in a manner that is mostly reactive and defensive. This phase of the struggle is, of course, a necessary one. It both exposes the weaknesses inherent in the opponent and clears the arena of spurious or unfounded assumptions. However, if we are to be true champions like Lewis who wrestle not just to protect ourselves but in order to win the prize, then we must follow our reactive defense with a proactive offense. Though we may—indeed, must—refer back to the traditional paradigm in our struggle with modernism, we must also have the vision to look forward toward a fuller, richer paradigm. This new paradigm will share the same essential nature as the traditional one, but it will be informed by and able to speak in the language of the modern one. In pursuit of this goal, I shall, both here and in the concluding sections of the chapters that remain, attempt to move the argument forward into a more offensive stance that not only broadens the scope of the argument but seeks to embody and incarnate that broader vision in a vital, original, concrete way. As before, I shall continue to use Lewis as my guide and example, but I shall also not constrain myself from offering my own Lewis-inspired analysis.

Challenge #1. Let us begin, then, by issuing a direct challenge to our opponent: Which paradigm, the traditional or the modern, has proven more effective in safeguarding those ideals and experiences and institutions that most make us human? Or, to take a specific case, which paradigm has provided the most solid foundation for preserving the integrity of those ethical standards upon which civil society rests, and in the absence of which society will eventually self-destruct? To answer this question, of course, we must first consider what is meant by a modernist ethics and how it relates to the bottom to top scheme described above. But to do so, we must look further back than the nineteenth century to that age and movement that first gave birth to the modernist paradigm: the eighteenth-century Enlightenment.

As one of the chief shapers of the Enlightenment, Immanuel Kant was troubled by a fear that the traditional mainstays of moral behavior were beginning to decay and even crumble. Though certainly a theist himself, Kant did not feel that divine revelation was a sufficiently strong base on which to risk the survival of personal and social morality. In response to this fear, Kant set himself a high task: to refound morality not on revelation but on purely rational, logical principles. This task, generally referred to as the Enlightenment Project, called for a radical shift from deduction to induction, from an old reliance on *a priori,* divinely revealed law codes such as the Ten Commandments and the Sermon on the Mount to a new reliance on systematic, logical proofs built upward from empirical observation. When asked why we consider a particular moral principle to be binding on us and our society, we need no longer refer back to an ancient commandment whose purported source was a divine fiat. Rather, we can justify our allegiance to the principle by constructing from the bottom up a pure structure of logical reasoning.

The textbook example of this process would refer us to what Kant dubbed the categorical imperative. In simple, schematic form, the categorical imperative works like this: Say you are trying to decide whether or not it is all right for you to steal a coat from a store. How are you to go about resolving this moral dilemma? Kant suggests that we first state our desire in the form of a maxim: It is all right for me to steal a coat from that store. Once you have done this, take your maxim and universalize it so that it may act as a general principle for all people: It is permissible for all people to steal any coat from any store they choose. Finally, take your universal maxim and hypothesize what would happen if all people obeyed this maxim. If you can do so without causing great danger or disruption to society, then you may enact your initial, personal maxim; however, if the application of that universal maxim (as in the case at hand) would lead to chaos, then it must be rejected. In essence, Kant is instructing his readers to follow the Golden Rule (Do unto others as you would have them do unto you), but with one vital difference. Whereas the latter rule rests squarely on revelation from above, the former relies on a logical process worked out from below.

It must be emphasized again that in formulating his categorical imperative and thus shifting the foundation of ethics from revelation to reason, Kant sincerely hoped to preserve morality for centuries to come. As it turned out, his modernist solution proved a failure. Whereas the traditional paradigm had lasted for two millennia, Kant's progressive, new-and-improved paradigm lasted less than a hundred years. By the close of the nineteenth-century, thinkers like Nietzsche had shattered Kant's seemingly impervious logic and opened the door to moral relativism. It is one of the greatest and saddest ironies in the history of philosophy. Kant, in the process of trying to preserve fixed standards of ethics, ended up opening a Pandora's box that paved the way for the debunking of those very standards he sought to save. Revelation, as it turned out, *was* a much surer foundation than reason. The seemingly unstable top to bottom structure ended up being stronger and more lasting than the supposedly stable bottom to top one. In a contest between the Tao and the Enlightenment Project, the former was clearly the victor.

—⚊—

Challenge #2. The modernist paradigm claims that its inductive approach to knowledge is more scientific and critical than the mostly deductive reasoning engaged in by Christians of the medieval and Renaissance periods. As stated earlier, many modernists would assert that whereas the conclusions reached via traditional deduction are finally subjective, those reached via empirical observation, as they are unrestrained by any prior assumptions, are essentially objective. But is this really true? Does the modernist paradigm really enable its practitioners to free themselves from all those troubling presuppositions that traditional thinkers took on faith? The answer, of course, is no.

When a Christian and a modern disagree over whether the parting of the Red Sea was a miracle, what is really at issue is not the specific form of reasoning, deduction or induction, that they used to arrive at their conclusion, but the underlying assumption about whether or not miracles occur in the first place. For it is a simple, indisputable fact that the majority of moderns just take for granted that the supernatural does not exist and that miracles are therefore impossible. They have not proven this assumption and rarely attempt to do so; they just accept it on faith as their given, their inductive *a priori*. The denial of the supernatural in general and of miracles in particular is part of their paradigm, part of their whole mental and emotional approach to the problems and puzzles of their day. Thus, when someone asks them to analyze the biblical story of the parting of the Red Sea, they begin by rejecting out of hand the possibility that the event was miraculous, at least in the sense of a divine intervention into the processes of nature and human history. Of course, once they reject without any logical or inductive reasoning to support the rejection the possibility that it *was* a miracle, they have no choice but to press on to find a natural cause for the event. And then once they have done so, they close the tautological loop and claim that their "scientific" explanation is just further proof that miracles don't happen.

Likewise, when adherents to the assumptions of higher criticism are asked to posit a composition date for a Gospel that includes Jesus' prediction that the Temple in Jerusalem will be destroyed, they will eventually arrive at the conclusion that the Gospel must have been written (or at least reached its final form) *after* 70 A.D. How do they arrive at this magic date? The answer is easy: Jesus' prediction about the Temple was accurately and literally fulfilled when the Romans razed the Temple to the ground in 70 A.D. And, since higher criticism accepts as truth the assumption that predictive prophecy does not occur, followers of it must end up by hook or by crook with a post-70 A.D. date. Now, of course, they will never admit that they are assuming *a priori* that predictive prophecy doesn't occur or that, in fact, their disbelief was the very *cause* of their textual analysis; they will claim rather that the *end point* of the textual analysis was the discovered "fact" that this prophecy was written after the event took place. Similarly, the accepted, "proven" conclusion that there were at least two, and probably three, Isaiahs (the second and third living well after the Jews returned to Jerusalem) does not rise up magically out of an objective, empirical, inductive study of the text. Rather, the conclusion is deductively reached by discounting the unacceptable fact—if one disbelieves in predictive prophecy—that the eighth-century B.C. Isaiah accurately predicts (45:1) the name of the Persian king (Cyrus) who would allow the sixth-century B.C. Jews to return to Jerusalem.

Many moderns who claim to reach their conclusions through pure induction are actually practicing a form of deduction in disguise. They claim to confine themselves to "just the facts," but their reading of those facts is conditioned by what they will and will not accept as scientific. All of this was best made clear to me when I stumbled upon a cartoon that featured an animated discussion between three friends: the first a Christian, the second an atheist, and the third an agnostic. The agnostic asks his two friends a simple question: What happened to Jesus' body? The Christian replies simply: God raised him from the dead. The atheist is more elaborate in his reply: A star ship from another galaxy happened to be flying over Palestine that day, and the captain decided to beam up the body and carry it back with him to his home world for biological analysis. The agnostic thinks a moment and then, pointing at the atheist, proclaims triumphantly, I shall go with the scientific explanation. The cartoon, for all its exaggeration, does not lie far from the truth. In our modern world, many interpreters of the Bible will sooner accept the most ludicrous "scientific" explanation than accept the possibility that a miracle occurred. In all fairness, it must be admitted that Christians have their givens as well, but then they are far more likely than the modernist is to confess to them, and they do not, in most cases, make exalted claims to be practicing an inductive, assumption-free form of inquiry.

Despite the claims of modern induction, Lewis writes in the first chapter of *Miracles* when it comes to the supernatural, "Seeing is not believing. . . . What we learn from experience depends on the kind of philosophy we bring to experience. . . . The result of our historical enquiries thus depends on the philosophical views [i.e., the *a priori* assumptions] which we have been holding before we even begin to look at the evidence." As always, Lewis Agonistes proves effective in the ring, for he not only understands the presuppositions of his opponents but knows how to flip those presuppositions (*and* his opponents) on their heads. Seeing is *not* believing. If a skeptic has already decided that miracles do not and cannot occur, then even if one should take place right in front of his nose, he would simply dismiss it as a coincidence, a natural anomaly, or, like Scrooge, as the result of "an undigested bit of beef, a blot of mustard, a crumb of cheese, a fragment of underdone potato."

—∽∾—

Challenge #3 follows in the wake of challenge #2, and takes up more fully the issue of God's divine intervention in the natural world. As Lewis devotes much of *Miracles* to demonstrating, part of the reason that the modern and the medieval disagree over the possibility of miracles is that the modern, who is naturalist in orientation, has a paltry and reductive view of what miracles are and how they function. The modernist sees a miracle as an aberration, a violation of the mechanistic laws of nature, and, as such, a logical contradiction. But that is only, Lewis explains in chapter 8, because the modern does not really understand what the laws of nature *are*. The modern speaks as if the laws of nature define fixed and standard outcomes, when, in fact, they merely describe a process.

Consider the law of inertia, which states that an object in motion will continue in motion unless acted upon by an outside force. What this law tells us is not that if we throw a ball, it will keep on moving through the air forever. It tells us rather that if, and only if, the flight of the ball is not impeded or interrupted by a second force, that the initial and constant force of inertia will keep it in motion. Of course (unless one is throwing the ball in outer space) a second force called gravity *will* interrupt its forward movement and "cancel out" the initial force of inertia. The result? The ball will fall to the ground. Has the law of inertia therefore been broken? Of course not. It has merely been suspended by the intervention of a second force.

If I hold a vase over my head in my right hand and then suddenly let go of the vase, the law of gravity dictates that the vase will fall to the ground and smash. Well, not exactly. The law does not predetermine that the vase will break, only that the natural process of gravitational attraction will draw the vase toward the ground. If I were just as suddenly to extend out my left hand and catch the vase before it smashed, the vase would be "saved." Have I broken the law of gravity? Of course not. I have merely *suspended* it by the intervention of an outside force. Naturalists and their behaviorist heirs like to use the image of a billiard table to illustrate the deterministic laws of cause and effect. If a ball is struck with a certain speed and at a certain angle and if the table has no flaws in it, the ball will always rebound in the same way. Well, yes, that is true, but only if all factors remain equal. What if, after the ball was hit, a stranger reached out his arms, grabbed the edges of the table, and began to shake? The answer is obvious. The normal course of events would be suspended, and a wholly new event would result, one that could not be predicted—at least not by someone whose consciousness is restricted to our temporal world of past, present, and future.

Believing in miracles does *not* mean believing that $2 + 2 = 5$. It means believing that there is a supernatural being (or at least force) in the universe that is capable of intervening in human events, suspending the laws of nature, and consequently altering the natural flow of cause and effect. Unfortunately, not even this answer will satisfy all those who cast doubt on the possibility of the miraculous. There are many theists and even Christians who, though they accept that God exists and that he has the power to intervene in human affairs, yet believe that this is something that God would simply not do. Paying homage to the Deistic watchmaker God who remains aloof from the affairs of the humans he created, they refuse to accept that God would engage in such lowbrow parlor tricks as parting the Red Sea or changing water into wine. It offends their delicate sense of order and propriety to even *think* that God would "mess around" with the natural order that he fashioned. It would be beneath his divine dignity, an affront to creation and to the self-evident modernist paradigm. It almost goes without saying that such people nearly always embrace a theistic evolutionary scheme in which God ignites the original Big Bang and then steps back to let natural laws do the rest.

The wrestler Lewis Agonistes won't have any of this. Yes, he admits, for the conventional minded, every miracle recorded in the Bible represents a break with decorum. But for those who have eyes to see and ears to hear, miracles are signs of a deeper unity that runs throughout every blade of grass, every human decision, every divine promise. The modernist balks at the biblical claim that the Incarnate Christ was crucified and buried and then rose again from the dead, and yet is not this same cycle replayed in every corner of the created world? Every year, the seasons spin round us in an endless parade of life, death, and rebirth. The seed must fall into the ground and be buried before it can sprout into a tree and bear fruit. The DNA from the parents descends into a sperm and an egg, is buried for nine months in a dark womb, and then resurrects into the light of a new life. Even our own self-centered and egocentric thoughts must be given over to death and buried if they are to resurrect into the mature qualities of a self-actualized adult. So Lewis in chapter 14 lists the various manifestations of this recurrent pattern, only to conclude, in keeping not with the modernist but the traditional paradigm, that the "pattern is there in Nature because it was first there in God. All the instances of which I have mentioned [and of which I have paraphrased] turn out to be but transpositions of the Divine theme into a minor key. . . . The total pattern, of which they are only the turning point, is the real Death and Re-birth: for certainly no seed ever fell from so fair a tree into so dark and cold a soil as would furnish more than a faint analogy to the huge descent and re-ascension in which God dredged the salt and oozy bottom of Creation."

Whose God, then, is too small and whose vision of joy, ethics, and miracles is the more paltry and reductive? The modernist paradigm has all but run its course, and though it has bequeathed us many luxuries and medical advances for which I am truly grateful, it has hardly left us wiser or richer or more humane. The answers to all the big questions (Who am I? Why am I here? What is my purpose? Am I of value?) can only come from above. Indeed, without that above, we can account for very little that is of lasting worth in ourselves and our lives. We need a broader vision, one that can break from mere convention, that can see the deeper pattern and that can discern the fuller purpose. We need a vision, in short, that the modernist paradigm is powerless to supply.

—m—

I mentioned above that the Freudians have a pat response for answering Lewis's argument by desire. They claim that all our highest desires, whether they be ethical, religious, or aesthetic, are the material products of a lower-order desire (one that *could* have evolved) that has been first repressed and then sublimated in another form. Great art is, like our daydreams, just another type of wish fulfillment. What we call love is merely a sublimated form of that instinctual lust which lies buried deep in our unconscious. The lust is the primary, originary, natural thing; love is but the artificial, socially acceptable form that lust takes when it is filtered through our elaborate system of psychological defense mechanisms.

As always, Lewis's critique of this Freudian critique succeeds in flipping on their heads the assumptions on which the modernist paradigm rests. Why, Lewis asks, must we say that love is a sublimation of lust? Is it not equally possible that lust is a falling away from love? Why must love be considered a projection from below, an evolution? May it not be rather an incarnation from above, a transposition from a heavenly key into an earthly one? Is not the universal human experience that of a search for higher things that goes terribly astray? Of a "looking for love" that goes awry and devolves into lust? We can only compromise on ideals that we already have; we can only pervert something that was at one time pure. If the clock is winding down, there must have been a time when someone wound it up. Freud would strand us in Plato's Cave, where what we think is real is but a mess of shadows and shadows of shadows. Lewis would help to lead us out of that cave and into that glorious light that is both our origin and our destiny.

In *The Silver Chair,* one of the seven Chronicles of Narnia, Lewis tells the tale of how two earth children, Eustace and Jill, and a Marshwiggle named Puddleglum make their way into the underground cavern of the Emerald Witch to rescue Prince Rilian, whom she has bewitched. The heroes succeed in finding Rilian and breaking his trance, but, as they prepare to leave the cavern, they are confronted by the Witch. They expect that she will try to kill them or at least put them in chains, but instead she throws some magic dust into the fire and begins to strum her mandolin in a slow, hypnotic fashion. Slowly, insidiously, she attempts to convince the four of them that there is no world of Narnia to escape to, that all there is is the underground world in which they now reside. Jill responds that the Witch's words are nonsense, that they have all seen the sun and that they know that the green land of Narnia is real.

"What is this sun of which you speak?" asks the Witch in a sweet voice.

"Well," Jill replies, "it is like a torch but much brighter and warmer. It hangs in the sky and sheds its light on all of Narnia."

"Does it now?" says the Witch, "Are you really so sure? I tell you that there is no such thing as a sun. You simply stared at a torch so long that you began to wonder what it would be like if that torch could expand to a hundred times its size and never run down or grow cold."

The Witch's words and her logic are clearly false and even insane; yet, as she continues to play, the children are seduced into believing that all they have known is a lie and an illusion, that the cave is all that there is.

They are saved in the end from the Witch's dangerous, self-destructive illusion by Puddleglum who, in an attempt to clear his head from the Witch's magic, shoves his foot into the fire. The pain brings him back to his senses, and he (in a paraphrase of Pascal's Wager) says that Narnia and her sun may not be real, but they are a darn sight better than the dark, meaningless world of the Witch's cavern. With that, the children remember who they are and what they know and reject the false paradigm of the Witch.

Our age, it could be argued, has not been as lucky as Eustace, Jill, Puddleglum, and Rilian. We are still trapped in the dark cavern of the Emerald Witch, convinced by her cunning lies and twisted logic that we and our world are to be defined by our base things and not by our transcendent ones. Like people in a dream, we spent much of the twentieth century being seduced by one false "ism" after another, and even gave our allegiance to a series of totalitarian systems from the extreme ends of the political spectrum. We gave up on the sun and began to base our beliefs, our ideals, and our dreams on a host of dim and dying torches. In a very real sense, we sold our souls for a mess of pottage and surrendered our divine inheritance for an underground cave.

There is still a way out and back up into the light of revelation, but we will have to wrestle for it, and, like Lewis Agonistes, be willing to knock down a paradigm or two.

3

Wrestling with the New Age

The Return to Paganism

Since the Enlightenment, the Western world has grown increasingly enamored of a modernist mind-set that privileges the physical over the spiritual, that looks to natural processes rather than divine intervention as the origin of all things, and that champions the sciences rather than the humanities as the most reliable source of truth. Indeed, as argued earlier, many moderns have so embraced this mind-set or paradigm that they have become materialists and naturalists: that is to say, they have reached the rather stunning conclusion that all there is in the universe is matter/nature. For such people, the spiritual and the supernatural simply do not exist. Everything—from the miracles of the Bible to answered prayers for physical healing to reports of ghostly visitations—is privy to a scientific explanation and can be reduced to a set of natural phenomena. (Just as post-Freudian psychology has moved inexorably from the humanities to the social sciences to the natural sciences, so have manifestations of the psyche also become grouped under the rubric "natural phenomena.")

What we have witnessed over the last two centuries is nothing less than the slow but incessant secularization of society. Even philosophy and religion, despite their essential links to the metaphysical, have been reduced to an anthropocentric, this-world pragmatism and ethics. What began as a desire to fashion separate spheres for the secular and the religious ("the separation of church and state," to invoke a phrase that continues to be misused and misinterpreted in our country) has led to a situation in which the spiritual has been increasingly downplayed, deauthorized, and even ridiculed. The secular and the mundane have gained ascendancy over the sacred and the holy; in many ways, the former have replaced the latter. Or, to put it another way, the secular has coopted and absorbed the sacred, so that we now speak of the "temples of science" or the "mysteries of physics" or the "miracle of the double helix." We end up with the ironic paradox of Carl Sagan, whose modernist mind-set forbids him from positing any supernatural purpose or divine handiwork in the universe, gazing up at the sky with a look of religious awe and wonder on his face ("billions and billions of stars").

The pendulum has indeed swung far in the direction of science, empiricism, and objectivity, and it was only a matter of time before this relentless swing toward secularization set off a counter-swing back toward the sacred. In the wake of a monolithic "action," one that asserts that everything is physical, has sprung up an equal and opposite "reaction," one that would assert, as odd as it sounds to our modernist-trained ears, that everything is spiritual. This reaction has surfaced in various different forms, but it has come (since the 1980s) to be referred to under a single all-inclusive heading: the New Age. And, under that collective name, it has begun to exert a wider and wider influence over a vast and growing number of Westerners who hail from every profession, ethnic background, and socioeconomic class.

Yes, the reaction was to be expected; the unchecked, headlong progress of Enlightenment thought could not help but breed its own antithesis. Nevertheless, its inevitability does not take away from the strangeness of it all. In the very midst of a modern, scientific, technological age that all but worships objective, observable facts and that prides itself on having risen above anything that remotely smacks of superstition, a veritable, bona fide resurgence of paganism has broken out. True, there have always been (in one form or another) horoscopes, tarot cards, and spirit mediums, but not since the ancient world has the West seen such a widespread, multifaceted interest in all aspects of occult wisdom and practice. Stonehenge, the Egyptian pyramids, Machu Picchu, Norse runes: all have attracted more and more fanatic attention, not as archeological oddities, as the Victorians viewed them, but as potential sources of spiritual and psychic power. While science presses ahead to unpack the human genome and to break the code of our DNA, masses of people hungry for knowledge of a more esoteric variety increasingly turn to radically unscientific sources: Indian spirit guides, Ouija boards, fortune tellers, biorhythms, and angels of every possible kind. In place of the scientific method, with its focus on controlled research and experimentation, a host of New Age disciplines have arisen that promise more direct access to truth and reality: transcendental meditation, Yoga, mantras, the martial arts, and a number of distinctly unpleasant diets.

The New Age umbrella is wide indeed; within its ambit lie a smorgasbord of beliefs and methods. Still, despite this diversity, all the various elements that make up the New Age paradigm may be traced back finally to a single, central element of paganism—pantheism. In contrast to polytheism (the belief in many gods), pantheism holds that everything is god (*pan* in Greek means "all"). In other words, all of nature is animated by a divine presence or force that pervades and moves through all things. This force is not a personal being like the God of the Bible who created the world and is separate from it; on the contrary, the god of pantheism *is* the world. The trees, the rivers, the animals, the heavenly bodies—all are but the eyes and ears and limbs of this amorphous, personless deity. And we humans who dwell in this animated universe are ourselves but broken pieces of that greater, unifying whole. Ralph Waldo Emerson captures part of this pantheistic vision when he refers to human beings as "gods in ruins," but it is Tom Joad in Steinbeck's *The Grapes of Wrath* who captures most fully, if unwittingly, the true essence of the New Age: "Maybe . . . a fella ain't got a soul of his own, but on'y a piece of a big one."

For the orthodox Christian, human beings belong to a species unique in the universe; we alone are the special creation of a single, distinct soul joined intimately (and *incarnationally*) to a single physical body. Even in heaven, the Bible asserts, we will be clothed in glorious resurrection bodies and will thus continue to exist as amphibian creatures who are neither solely physical (like the animals) nor solely spiritual (like the angels). Modernism, by taking the soul out of the equation and reinterpreting mankind in solely physical, material terms, essentially reduced the human race to the level of the animal kingdom. The New Age, rather than return to the Christian view, embraced the other extreme and strove to make angels of us all. For the neopagan, it is not the soul that is an illusion (as it is, finally, for the modernist) but the body. All physical things (whether they be the bodies of plants, animals, or human beings) are merely fleeting, disposable coverings for that one, great divine force that is the soul of all.

We refer to New Agers as neopagans, and rightly so since the majority of their beliefs *do* parallel ancient Greco-Roman teachings, but most of them, when it comes right down to it, know very little of our classical pagan heritage. It is to the East they look for guidance, to Tibetan monks, Hindu swamis, Zen masters, and martial arts gurus. They are not so much reactionaries in search of the pagan roots of Western culture as they are rebels against Western Enlightenment thought (which they define as complicit with, rather than opposed to, traditional Christian thought). They seek an alternative to modernism, a new orientation that is anti-Western and antirational, and they find it in the mystical storehouses of India, China, and Japan. In this sense they are not so much premodern as they are postmodern, displaced Westerners who have lost their faith in the structures of logical, rational, scientific thought.

In the unified spiritual order of pantheism, they have found instead a counter-structure that is really, in its essence, a structureless structure. It promises to free them from all material limits and boundaries. As such, it is no surprise that New Agers gravitate toward anything that is linked to or rises up out of a pantheistic worldview, what the Germans call a *Weltanschauung*. Thus, most devotees of the New Age express a belief in the traditional Eastern doctrine of reincarnation, a teaching that views the soul as passing through a series of physical forms the way a human body puts on and discards an ever shifting array of shirts and shoes and undergarments. At first glance, this teaching might seem to affirm a faith in progressive growth and change, but that, too, is an illusion. For the final goal of reincarnation is not to attain that perfection of personhood that the Christian doctrine of the resurrection body promises, but to escape from the wheel of reincarnation (or *samsara*) and ascend to an unconscious, personless state, Nirvana, that transcends both pleasure and pain. Or to put it in terms of a phrase more familiar to Western ears, the ultimate end of the soul's journey is to be reunited with the One Soul out of which it came.

—⚉—

Such are the mind-set and some of the more common manifestations that underlie and define the New Age movement. But why, we still must ask, are so many in the West flocking to it in unprecedented numbers? I've already suggested above the basic motivation, a rejection of the excesses of modernism and materialism, but if we are to answer with Lewis's help the challenge of the New Age, then we must attempt to be more specific. More importantly, if we are to accept the New Age not as an all-out threat to the church but as an opportunity to reach a multitude of souls hungry for spiritual truth, then we must learn to identify, understand, and sympathize with the desires and yearnings that drive these passionate neopagans.

The motives we seek, of course, already lie implicitly before us in the very nature of that pantheistic mind-set that the New Ager so eagerly embraces. Unity, in a word, is what he seeks, but not the simple unity of being part of a social club or a charitable organization or even a family. It is a higher and deeper kind of unity that allows one to experience a sense of connection and purpose in, through, and with all living things. It is the desire to feel and believe that one lives in a sympathetic universe, one in which the turnings of the seasons, the phases of the moon, and the orbits of the planets have something to do with us. The New Ager longs to feel that the universe is not merely his house but his home, but he cannot do so within the Western *Weltanschauung,* for the modern world has killed the heavens. Just as the vivisectionist inevitably kills the animal that he is studying, so modern science, in its quest to understand the cosmos, has simultaneously emptied it of life, mystery, and meaning. Ironically, though the modernist paradigm rests on the belief that human life evolved out of nature, it nevertheless cuts us off from that very nature that it claims gave us birth. Indeed, the overriding goal of science and technology as C. S. Lewis reveals it in *The Abolition of Man* and *That Hideous Strength* is to sever us completely from any dependence on nature, to lift us up and out of that very seasonal cycle that the New Ager longs to feel a part of.

Here then is the problem. Modern New Agers desperately yearn to encounter beauty, wonder, and holiness in the world around them. But the modern world has killed the heavens, and, alas, the church has performed the funeral. Orthodox Christians of the twenty-first century may resist the evolutionary mind-set of post-Enlightenment science and may hold to a firm belief in the miraculous and the supernatural, but they, like the modern scientist, are nevertheless suspicious of New Age "nature talk." Most Christians of today share science's goal of overcoming nature and strongly oppose anything that remotely suggests a return to pagan superstition. We'll brook no slippery talk of spirits that roam the woods and destinies that are written in the stars, and, though we convince ourselves that our objection to such things is purely doctrinal, the fact is that we really reject such talk because it offends our modern, Western, scientific sensibilities. Sadly, this dynamic *between* Christians and New Agers often rises up (in a different but parallel form) *within* Christianity itself. Thus, many in the reformed and dispensational traditions will attack pentecostalism in the *name* of sound doctrine, when, in fact, their deeper and primary motive for doing so is that the charismatic worship style offends their sense of order, propriety, and rational behavior.

What the New Ager perceives as the staleness and rigidity of Christian doctrine cannot compete with the awe and beauty of myth; Christ pales for him when held up against Balder, Osiris, and Adonis. The mystery and wonder of the *Iliad,* the Greek tragedies, and the Hindu *Vedas* and *Upanishads* seem lacking in the Bible; the warmth and inclusiveness of pantheism seem absent in the cold, exclusivist creeds of the church. In search of a holistic connection to nature below and the heavens above, the New Ager finds (*both* in science and the church) a black-and-white view of reality that would cut him off from both and that would leave him stranded on the outside of a gate that is very narrow and very forbidding.

There are two basic ways of challenging nonbelievers to embrace Christianity. One way is to *scare* the hell out of them through fire-and-brimstone sermons that paint in lurid detail the punishment for sin and heresy. The other is to *coax and draw them in* by introducing them to the glory of the Father, the love of the Son, and the communion of the Holy Spirit. The former succeeds by a process of a division, by swiftly bringing down that two-edged sword that cuts to the very bone. The latter appeals to their most intimate longings and yearnings, what Lewis calls "the argument by desire," and fashions a golden pathway along which the would-be pilgrim can follow the divine intimations to their proper goal in Christ.

As a Christian church, we have done a fine job exposing the many heresies latent in New Age beliefs and practices: of rational apologists we have no lack. But how adept are we at identifying and meeting the deeper spiritual needs that impel the devotees of the New Age? If we are to win back the neopagans, we need to rediscover our awe at the majesty of God and his Creation, an awe that has little to do with the modern warfare over worship styles and everything to do with that breathless sense of the numinous that we first encountered in the nursery when a timeless tale from mythology or folklore or legend ushered us into the world of faerie.

The Medieval Net Was Wider Than Our Own

The answer to reaching the New Age lies in part behind us, in a concerted effort to recapture an older, medieval worldview that guided Europe for a thousand years and that continued to exert its influence throughout the Renaissance. And, in our pursuit of that vital road backward, we can hope for no better guide than C. S. Lewis.

New Agers, as we have seen, yearn to live in a sympathetic universe. They search in vain to find it in the modern church, and then turn to find it elsewhere. But had they lived in the Age of Dante, they need have looked no further than the doors of the Catholic Church. For there they would have encountered a conception of the universe, a cosmology, that found life, meaning, and aesthetic design in the heavens. The root meaning of the Greek word *cosmos* is "ornament" (as in our modern word "cosmetics"), and to the classical, medieval, and Renaissance mind, the universe was nothing more or less than the ornament of God. In the heavens, the stargazer who had eyes to see could perceive the same order, balance, and harmony, albeit on a lesser scale, that existed in the mind of God.

There are several books available that map out the medieval cosmological model, most notably Arthur O. Lovejoy's *The Great Chain of Being* and E. M. W. Tillyard's *The Elizabethan World Picture,* but the best of them was written by Lewis himself. Published posthumously in 1964 and composed of lectures that Lewis delivered at Cambridge, *The Discarded Image* lays out in exquisite detail the medieval model that undergirds Dante's *Divine Comedy.* With his usual mix of scholarly precision and imaginative insight, Lewis allows us to see and feel the cosmos as the medievals themselves felt it; the experience is breathtaking.

Around a fixed, central earth, a series of nine concentric spheres wheeled and spun in perfect circular orbits. Embedded in these crystalline spheres were, in ascending order, the seven heavenly bodies (the moon, Mercury, Venus, the Sun, Mars, Jupiter, Saturn), the fixed stars, and the *primum mobile* (or first mover) which set all the other spheres in motion and was itself set in motion by God (the unmoved mover). As the spheres moved through the heavens, the differing pitches of their orbits produced a heavenly music so refined and ethereal that our dull, earthly ears could not hear it.

As Lewis describes it in *The Discarded Image,* the medieval model was one that wholly satisfied, one that struck its contemplators with all the power and beauty of an epic poem; *their* universe was not a lifeless object like ours, but a vital, animated presence that could not only be appreciated but loved. Indeed, in accordance with the ancient principle of plenitude (or fullness) the medievals believed that the heavens (or "outer space" as we moderns call it) were not a cold, dead vacuum, but a warm, dazzling field throbbing with life. Even the spheres themselves were not, as it might at first seem, automatic, mindless gears in a cosmic machine; quite the contrary, each of them was impelled by an intelligence that moved its sphere out of love for the Creator. Whereas our age *reasons* that the vast actions and interactions of the cosmos are best defined in terms of abstract *principles* such as the laws of gravity and of thermodynamics, the medievals *saw* a more personal universe whose intricate movements, like those of a dance, were set in motion and choreographed by divine *influence.*

Medieval poets like Dante and Chaucer (and Renaissance poets like Shakespeare, Donne, and Milton) lived in a sympathetic universe, one in which all the parts were related, in which the stars *did* have something to do with us and the Creator was not a mere uninvolved watchmaker. Today, as we have seen, any notion that we and our world might be influenced by the movements and arrangements of the heavenly bodies is relegated to the fringes of the New Age; in the days before Enlightenment skepticism (and, I'm afraid, Protestant rationalism) unweaved the rainbow and stripped the cosmos of its mystery, the church was wide enough and, dare we say it, enlightened enough to find truth in the astrological speculations of the ancient pagan world. This is not to say that the Catholic Church condoned horoscopes and fortune-telling, but they did accept as a general rule the meaningfulness and interrelatedness of the changing world below and the more perfect world above. If, asChristians say they believe, God fashioned both us and our universe, is it not right that there should exist some sympathy between the two? Was it not a heavenly body, after all, that led the pagan Wise Men to the Christ child?

For the medievals, it was not the laws of Newtonian physics but what Dante calls "the love that moves the sun and the other stars" that gives the cosmos its shape and its integrity. We are all, to borrow another Dantean image, like ships seeking to find our eternal port, our proper and assigned place vis-à-vis God. All in the universe is free to follow its instincts, yet nothing is haphazard. In all things, there is order and purpose. Every heavenly being (from seraphim to cherubim to archangel), every human, every animal, even every plant has its place in that Great Chain of Being that stretches downward from God to the lowest form of inorganic life. Indeed, one of the hallmarks of the medieval model, Lewis argues, was its ability to integrate a vast amount of speculative material (both pagan and Christian, philosophical and theological, scientific and poetic) into a unified system. Out of a Chaos of Forms and Ideas, the medievals (like the God they worshiped) forged a unified system in which order and hierarchy were the rule. And yet, as difficult as it may seem for us inhabitants of a democratic, antiaristocratic world to believe, that order was personal and intimate and that hierarchy just, reasonable, and human in the most exalted sense.

In the biographical material, we explored how Owen Barfield helped the young, pre-Christian Lewis to break out of his chronological snobbery and look afresh at that medieval Christian world he had been too quick to dismiss as dark and unenlightened. Barfield may also have been the one who helped Lewis to link the abandonment of the medieval model, not merely to changes in technology (i.e., better telescopes), but to a vital shift in the way we perceive the universe. In his seminal study, *Saving the Appearances,* Barfield argues that whereas moderns hold an objective view of nature and the universe, those who lived in the classical and medieval period saw their world in subjective terms. We moderns look upon things that lie outside us as existing apart from us, as removed objects, things to be studied from a distance. Our forbears did not see it the same way. They and the objects around them were linked in what Barfield terms "original participation." The universe did not exist as an object apart from them, but existed in and together with their perceptions of it. Medieval cosmology marked an attempt to "save the appearances" (the phrase does not originate with Barfield; it appears in the works of writers from Aristotle to Milton). It sought to make sense of that vast and complex universe that stretched out before the wondering eyes of man in all its awe and beauty. But somewhere along the road to the modern, scientific world, we cut the universe loose from our perceptions of it and thus banished ourselves from original participation.

This distinction between a subjective and an objective view of nature can help us to understand why Galileo provoked great opposition when he argued for a heliocentric (sun-centered) universe, while Copernicus, who had made the same claim a generation earlier, escaped persecution. In presenting his revised cosmological model, Copernicus remained firmly within the subjective mind-set; his was but another of many attempts to save the appearances (indeed, a few of the ancient cosmographers had themselves attempted to arrange the universe along a heliocentric model). But Galileo strove to push European scientific and astronomical thought into an objective phase. His theories were not put forward as another way to make sense of the heavens and our relationship to it, but as a statement, once and for all, of what the cosmos actually *was,* apart from our perceptions of it. Today, of course, if an astronomer were to suggest a return to original participation, that scientist would be quickly ridiculed and encouraged to recant. An astronomer who refused would not be burned at the stake—liberal enlightenment thought *has* taught us some very good lessons. Rather, the stargazer would be shrugged off by the academy and the church alike as just another crazy New Ager.

The church cannot reach the New Ager because it cannot understand how New Age neopagans understand the world around them. As I have already suggested above, our age is powerless to answer the New Age critique of modern science and religion because so few of us know how it *feels* to live in a universe that is alive with its Father's presence. But Lewis, who steeped himself in that more vibrant, Old European world that stretches from the ancient Greeks to Samuel Johnson, knew what it was like to see the dance of the stars and hear the music of the spheres. Indeed, in the address he delivered to inaugurate his new position as chair of Medieval and Renaissance Literature at Cambridge, "De Descriptione Temporum" (anthologized in *Selected Literary Essays*), he compared himself to a dinosaur, to one who still believed, embodied, and felt in his bones the ideals, the values, and the worldview that invigorate the work of Christian poets from Dante to Milton.

If we are to broaden our witness to those in the New Age movement, then we must do the same. We must discover, as Dante discovered, how we ourselves fit in the greater weave of the cosmos, and we must learn to sing along with St. Francis of Assisi our own Canticle of Brother

Sun. We must learn how to direct the New Ager back to the wonders of a fully realized Christian universe, and, in the process, revive as well our own latent capacity for wonder.

—∞—

But this renewal of wonder represents only the first defensive move in our Lewis-inspired wrestling match with the New Age. Once we have dealt with the New Age reaction against the church's coldness and objectivity, we must still battle its critique of its exclusivism. Of course, here we spar with a more dangerous foe. Christianity is, after all, a religion that has its share of dualisms—light/dark, angel/devil, heaven/hell—but that, nonetheless, rests on a core claim that Jesus alone is the Way, the Truth, and the Life. There are a number of doctrines that are non-negotiable, including the Trinity, the Incarnation, the Atonement, and the Resurrection, and the Gospel promises salvation only to those who are in Christ.

Nevertheless, Christianity's exclusive focus on the triune nature of God and on the unique person and work of Jesus Christ does not necessitate its enthronement as that monolithic, black-and-white religion that the New Ager often confuses it for. Indeed, I would submit, Christianity is *not* the only truth. If it were, that would lead us to the false conclusion that all religions and cultures that exist outside the walls of the church are made up of lies and darkness. No, Christianity is not the only truth, but it is the only *complete* truth. The distinction is vital. According to the latter phrase, there *are* elements of truth in all religions and cultures, but only in the person of Jesus Christ do we find Truth revealed in all its divine fullness. Like the famous statue of him poised on that lofty mountain in Rio, the eternal, Incarnate Christ stands at the top of the hill with his arms spread wide, inviting all pilgrims, including New Agers, to ascend. There are many ways around that hill, and many never make it to the top, but to those who persist to the end and whose hearts yearn for God, the truth and presence of Christ will be revealed. Of course, once they see that revelation, they may choose to reject it or dismiss it as an illusion. But if they embrace it, they will find that all their deepest longings and desires were but a prelude and a preparation for the full and perfect revelation that is in Christ.

Many orthodox Christians, especially those like myself who define themselves as evangelicals, would dispute that people in religions and cultures that lie outside of Christianity can, on the basis of their limited wisdom and their innate yearnings, make a partial move toward Christ. But is this not the message of the journey of the Magi? The Magi were not Jews—they were most likely Zoroastrians from Persia. They did not have access, at least as far as we know, to the Hebrew Scriptures. But they yearned for truth, and they sought that truth in the only way they knew how—by studying the stars and their sacred motions. They followed those stars and their yearnings, and were led, step by weary step, to the Christ child. Once they arrived, they could have rejected the child and sought something more abstract, more esoteric, but they did not. Rather, they found that their study of the stars had prepared them to discover and embrace the concrete reality of the babe in the manger, and they accepted him.

Is it not possible that there are uncounted numbers of New Age magi out there whose espousal of nature worship, Eastern mysticism, and occult wisdom is a manifestation, not of rebellion, but of a sincere if misguided attempt to seek a truth and an intimacy that, though they do not yet know it, only Christ can fulfill? Are they not like the Samaritan woman at the well (John 4), whose serial monogamy disguised a deeper need for acceptance and intimacy that only the living water of Christ could fully satisfy? She, like her fellow Samaritans, worshiped on the wrong mountain and in the wrong way, yet she still knew, like the Magi, that a Messiah was coming and eagerly received him when he made himself known to her. The Roman centurion, Cornelius (Acts 10), did not possess the Law or the Prophets, but he was a good and righteous man whose piety was sincere. God saw his heart and knew his sincerity, and he sent Peter to guide Cornelius up that hill on whose summit stands Christ and Christ alone. Paul's great success as an evangelist was predicated in part on his ability to speak to pagans in their own language. He did not, as the Jerusalem Church would have had him do (Galatians 2), force his Gentile converts to become Jews first and then Christians.

Rather, he invited them, as they were, to receive Christ as the culmination of their spiritual journey.

Such is the import of his speech before the Areopagus in Athens, as recorded by Luke in Acts 17:22–31. As he wended his way through the marketplace of the city, Paul noticed that the Athenians had an idol or temple dedicated to every conceivable god. Among these shrines, his eyes fell upon an altar dedicated to an unknown God. Seizing on this serendipitous connection between the pagan question and the Christian answer, Paul requested a hearing before the council and immediately confronted them with their cryptic altar. "What you have worshiped without knowing," he assured them, "I will now proclaim to you as known." And, with that as his cultural link, Paul went on to open the eyes of the council to God's wider plan and purpose. The God who created the world and divided the people of the earth into separate nations is an eternal, invisible God who does not dwell in temples made by human hands. He is an active God who reaches out to all people and who has set the times for every tribe and nation. Indeed, he did so in hopes that those very groups would yearn for his presence and grope after his truth. And he decreed that their strivings would not be in vain, for he is not far from any of us: in him we live and move and have our being. As even the poets of the pagans understood, we are his offspring. But now, that same God has declared a day (Today!) when all will be judged by a man appointed of God, a man whose universal authority was made clear by God's raising him from the dead.

Most of the men who listened that day were not as noble as the Magi or open as the Samaritan or pious as Cornelius. Wisdom was something they picked at and played with, and so they rejected Paul's message. But there *were* some who believed, who recognized that the man of whom Paul spoke, Jesus Christ, was what they long had sought in their gnostic scrolls and sacred mysteries. Paul had won them over, not by exposing their heresies, but by inviting them to finish their spiritual pilgrimage, by revealing to them that, joy of joys, at the end of their search there awaited something real, whole, and lasting. Indeed, I would argue that Jesus himself made the same invitation to a group of Greek pagans who conveyed to him through Andrew and Philip their desire to

WRESTLING WITH THE NEW AGE

meet him (John 12:20–22). I strongly suspect that these Greeks, who were clearly interested in both the religious rites of the Jews and in the teachings and person of Jesus, were initiates of the Eleusinian mysteries: an ancient cultic religion that worshiped the seasonal cycle and the dying and rebirth of both the grape and the wheat. This is Jesus' response to the Greeks: "The hour is come, that the Son of man should be glorified. Verily, verily, I say unto you, Except a [grain] of wheat fall into the ground and die, it abideth alone: but if it die, it bringeth forth much fruit" (12:23–24). The saying is a unique one and employs a metaphor that Jesus uses only here. To a Jew, the message would be a cryptic one, but to an initiate of the Eleusinian mysteries it could have only one meaning: that which you have long worshiped as a myth and a ritual I now proclaim to you as a historical reality.

Jesus' metaphor brings us, by a somewhat circuitous route, back to C. S. Lewis whose conversion, as we saw earlier, did not occur until he realized via his all-night walk with Tolkien that Jesus Christ, far from being one in a long line of mythic dying gods, was, in fact, the myth come true. Indeed, one of Lewis's greatest services as an apologist was to demonstrate that in the person of Christ we encounter a figure whose life, death, and resurrection does not stand in opposition to the mythic heroes of paganism, but presents instead a literal, historical fulfillment of what all those earlier myths were really about. Or, to put it another way, just as Christ came not to abolish the Law but to fulfill it, so he came not to put an end to myth but to take all that is most essential in the myth up into himself and make it real. In "Myth Became Fact," a seminal essay anthologized in *God in the Dock,* Lewis strikes his blows for this argument:

> The heart of Christianity is a myth which is also a fact.
> The old myth of the Dying God, *without ceasing to be
> myth,* comes down from the heaven of legend and
> imagination to the earth of history. It *happens*—at a
> particular date, in a particular place, followed by
> definable historical consequences. We pass from a Balder
> or an Osiris, dying nobody knows when or where, to a
> historical Person crucified (it is all in order) *under*

Pontius Pilate. By becoming fact it does not cease to be
myth: that is the miracle. . . . God is more than god, not
less: Christ is more than Balder, not less. We must not be
ashamed of the mythical radiance resting on our
theology. We must not be nervous about "parallels" and
"Pagan Christs": they *ought* to be there—it would be a
stumbling block if they weren't. We must not, in false
spirituality, withhold our imaginative welcome. If God
chooses to be mythopoeic—and is not the sky itself a
myth—shall we refuse to be *mythopathic?*

Could we understand fully all that is suggested in this passage and apply
it to our reactions to and interactions with our neopagan neighbors, we
would find ourselves far more able to address the needs of those who
continue to flock to the New Age. As biblical, credal Christians, we are
quick to say with Paul that we are not ashamed of the gospel; let that
boldness include not only the doctrinal elements of the Good News, but
its mythic elements as well.

Jesus represents in his personhood not only the goal and culmination of the Jewish Law and Prophets, but of all the deepest philosophical, theological, and aesthetic yearnings of humanity. The writer
who best understood this movement from pagan to Christian, Dante,
was also the one who most fully embodied in his work the medieval
model. When Dante sat down to write his *Divine Comedy* and considered whom he would choose as his guide through hell and purgatory, he
did not choose, as we would expect, Peter or Paul or Augustine or
Aquinas. Rather, he chose a pagan poet, Virgil, who died two decades
before the birth of Christ. He did so because he discovered in Virgil's
writings, particularly the *Aeneid* and the Fourth Eclogue, the seeds and
the shadows of greater truths that would soon be revealed through
Christ, the Bible, and the Catholic Church. In Dante's mind and in that
of the Middle Ages in general Virgil was a sort of proto-Christian, one
whom God used to prepare the pagan world for his coming. Indeed, in
the Fourth Eclogue, written about forty years before the birth of Christ,
Virgil speaks cryptically of the coming of a divine child who will bring

universal peace. The poem reads like a prophetic chapter from Isaiah, and the medievals read it as such.

But Virgil represents something more for Dante. In the allegory of the *Divine Comedy,* Virgil symbolizes the best that human reason can achieve. He cannot lead Dante all the way to God—for that, Dante must be turned over to Beatrice, the representative in the poem of divine grace—but he can offer him a good beginning; he can lead him, in fact, to the very gates of Eden, that place that was meant to be our proper home. Virgil's wisdom alone cannot save, but then neither can that of Moses or David or Ezekiel. Yes, the Jewish prophets had access to a direct form of revelation that was not vouchsafed to the pagan Virgil, but Virgil did glimpse *something* of the truths waiting to be brought to light in the person and teachings of Christ. Perhaps Virgil saw very dimly in a stained and distorted mirror, but he *did* see. When Michelangelo painted his masterpiece of sacred history on the ceiling of the Sistine Chapel, he included, among the prophets of Israel, the pagan Sibyls of ancient Rome. Likewise, in the mystery plays of the Middle Ages that enacted the stories of the Bible in a hearty vernacular the Sibyls often appear near the end of a long line of Old Testament figures who speak their prophecies of the coming Messiah. For Dante, Michelangelo, and the anonymous authors of the mystery plays, not to mention C. S. Lewis, the wisdom of the pagan is like a candle that lights our way through the dark night but then is blown out (or, better, absorbed) when morning finally comes, and the bright sun of God's Word, both Christ and the Bible, shines forth its light. According to church tradition, when Christ was born, all the pagan prophets from the Roman Sibyls to the Greek Oracle of Delphi ceased to speak.

Viewed in isolation, the above statement might seem to suggest that since we now live on the other side of the Cross, there is no further need for candles. But this is not necessarily the case. Christ is always building his church, and the divine child is ever being born anew in Bethlehem. The dark forces of paganism may be gone, but they have been replaced in our day by the even darker forces of a monolithic materialism that would squelch even the tiniest spark of spiritual truth. In this shrouded, predawn world, many, though they yearn for divine light, are unprepared to gaze into the face of the sun. For these, perhaps, the New Age serves as a candle lighting their way and preparing their eyes for a greater light to come. Yes, for many in the New Age, the candle is seized as a conscious substitute for the Christian sun; but it is my firm belief that there are just as many who would trade in their candle if they could only be shown that the sun is the Son whom they truly seek, and that that sun, to paraphrase Lewis, is more than the candle, not less.

The early church, faced with the daunting task of converting a pagan empire into a Christian one, understood this dynamic, and it led them to make some decisions that now appear suspect—if not heretical—to modern, post-Reformation believers. I speak in particular of their decision to proclaim December 25 as the official birth date of Christ. Although nobody really knows *when* Christ was born, we can probably say with some certainty that he was not born in December, for the shepherds would not have been keeping watch on the hills if he were. Why then did the early church choose December 25 to celebrate the divine birth? The answer is an instructive one. The pagans of the ancient Roman world were already used to celebrating a religious holiday, the winter solstice, around December 25. In fact, at least two celebrations converged at that time of the year: the birthday of the unconquered sun (which was linked to the influential and widespread cult of Mithras), and the Saturnalia (an anarchic, Mardi Gras-like time of freedom and plenty that hearkened back to an earlier, Edenic golden age). As the sun was a fit symbol for the light and glory of Christ, as Mithras was one of those mythical dying and rising gods who prefigure the historical Jesus, and as the Saturnalia expressed a longing to return to a prefallen world, it seemed only appropriate that the Incarnation, in which all three of these things reached their ultimate fulfillment, should be celebrated at the same time of year.

For theologians such as Tertullian, the fact that the cult of Mithras bore stunning similarities to the birth, death, and resurrection of Christ was clear proof that it had been invented by the devil to deceive the early Christians. Those in the church who set the date of Christmas, I would argue, saw it differently. Why change or eradicate the religious devotion of the pagans, when that same devotion could be rechannelled in a proper direction? Why not show them that the birth of the babe in the manger marked not the antithesis but the true and full embodiment of their spiritual yearnings? Why not let the annual return of December 25 be a constant reminder that in the dark streets of Bethlehem there once shown, not the rays of the unconquerable sun, but the "everlasting light" of the Creator of the sun? That in a moment of supreme magic, "the hope and fears of all the years" were met, fused, and consummated.

No, the dating of Christmas is not an example, as it is for many Protestants, of how the Catholic Church allowed the purity of biblical doctrine to be compromised and watered down by an infusion of pagan beliefs and practices. It represents, rather, a higher kind of evangelism that would break down the dividing wall between Jew and Gentile, Christian and pagan, and build in its place a royal road leading up the sides of Mount Zion to that sacred city, the New Jerusalem, and to the resplendent Lord of that city: the Unconquerable Sun (and Son) of Righteousness.

In chapter 10 of his *Reflections on the Psalms* (which covers much of the same ground as I have in the preceding paragraphs), Lewis offers an illustration to help us understand the relationship between inchoate yearnings unguided by direct revelation and the object that is the real but unknown source of those yearnings:

> If a man who knew only England and had observed
> that, the higher a mountain was, the longer it retained
> the snow in early spring, were led on to suppose a
> mountain so high that it retained the snow all the year
> round, the similarity between his imagined mountain
> and the real Alps would not be merely a lucky accident.
> He might not know that there were any such mountains
> in reality. . . . But if that man ever saw the Alps he would
> not say, "What a coincidence." He would be more likely
> to say, "There! What did I tell you?"

It is this very response (one that the early church hoped to elicit from the pagan worshipers of Mithras and the sun) that we should seek to inspire in the devotees of the New Age. In our wrestling with the postmodern challenge of neopaganism, we must learn to discern the difference between inward desire and outward practice, and seek to realign the two in such a way that spiritual desire finds its final and natural outlet in the person of Christ and the fellowship of the church. Many of the martial arts teach their disciples how to use an opponent's strength and force against him. Rather than resist the New Age passion for all that is spiritual, holy, and sacred, let us use it as the fulcrum with which to lift the New Ager into the waiting arms of a holistic and revivified church whose renewed vision and capacity for wonder can take in the very heavens themselves.

Rehabilitating the Medieval Model

Indeed, the solution to the New Age crisis—and it *is* a crisis, not a threat—lies, in many ways, behind us. If we are to be successful evangelists in the ripe fields of neopaganism, we must recapture that wider Dantean scope that can perceive the progression from Virgil to Beatrice, reason to grace, pagan to Christian, and that can also conceive of the cosmos as a majestic pendant hung round the neck of the Creator. But we cannot stop here. As discussed earlier, the reactive defense that sends us backward to the medieval model must be followed by a proactive offense that carries that model into the wrestling arena of the twenty-first century.

Fortuitously, here, too, Lewis Agonistes can be our guide and model. For Lewis, it was not enough merely to understand the medieval model; its message had to be updated and transported to the modern world. And Lewis, as both scholar and artist, found a dual way to accomplish this task through the mediation of his academic work and his fictional tales. In the former arena, Lewis strove to revive the medieval model by forcing his readers Christian and secular alike to see and to acknowledge that the medievals were neither so unenlightened, nor are we so scientific and objective, as we would like to believe. In the latter, he took the medieval model and embodied it in two series of novels: the space trilogy and the Chronicles of Narnia.

The fact of the matter is, most Westerners, whether they dropped out of high school or earned a graduate degree, have a skewed view of the Middle Ages and of what those who lived in it felt and believed.

Employing propagandistic language that was fashioned, not, as most suppose, by Renaissance thinkers like Petrarch and Machiavelli, but by such French Enlightenment thinkers as Voltaire and Diderot, moderns continue to speak of the medieval world as a Dark Age of ignorance, superstition, and obscurantism. Science, rationality, and technology, we like to think, have freed us from all that medieval doom and gloom. And on what do we rest our claim of moral and intellectual superiority? We could come up with fancy-sounding justifications, but when it comes right down to it, most of us ground our patronizing attitude on a single well-known "fact": Those poor medievals were so blind that they thought they lived on a flat earth!

Lewis's goal of reviving the medieval model begins precisely here with the debunking of a very old Enlightenment "smear campaign." Contrary to widespread popular and academic opinion, he explains that the medievals did *not* believe that the earth was flat. Yes, it was believed until Copernicus that the earth was at the center of the universe, but all educated medievals knew that it was round, a fact that Lewis proves in *The Discarded Image* by quoting numerous scholars prior to 1500 A.D. from Aristotle to Ptolemy to Aquinas, all of whom were well aware of the shape of the earth—and as for the uneducated, Lewis adds, most of them just didn't think about it at all. Columbus's contemporaries ridiculed his plan, not because they thought the world was flat and he thought it was round, but because they thought that Columbus had grossly underestimated the size of the globe, which, in fact, he had. Furthermore, again contrary to entrenched modernist belief, the recent "discovery" of the vastness of space is not, in fact, a discovery at all. Numerous ancient authorities, Boethius in particular, asserted not only the vastness of space but the comparative spatial insignificance of the earth.

Neither the ancients nor the medievals were fools. They had eyes that saw, and they used them quite well. But what they saw and, more importantly, *how* they saw were vastly different from what and how we see today. True, we cannot and should not simply return to the medieval model; science *has,* Lewis freely admits, disproven such medieval assumptions as the circular movements of the spheres and the unchangeable perfection of the heavens. Nevertheless, this does not validate any smug self-assurance that we are all right and they were all wrong, an attitude that still persists among many Christians, Protestants *as well as* Catholics, and that is closely related to our discomfort with and rejection of the New Age.

We must accept once and for all, argues Lewis in the final chapter of *The Discarded Image,* that our modern cosmological model is just that, a model: one that can, at any moment, be wiped away by some new scientific discovery. We laugh at the medievals for their quaint metaphorical notion that heavenly "bodies" move through celestial influence, but is such a view any more metaphorical than our notion that all objects "obey"—using a term suggestive of the way good citizens follow our society's laws—the laws of gravity? When it comes to models, you see, we find what we're looking for, just as in court, the lawyer's questions often determine the shape of the testimony. We seek, as the medievals sought, to save the *appearances*—to fashion a model that would explain the nature of the observed universe. If the medievals were guilty of shaping their model in accordance with their love for pageantry and hierarchy, then we are no less guilty of shaping ours along legal, democratic lines. All people, whether ancient or modern, medieval or enlightened, have their presuppositions, and they cannot help but bring those presuppositions with them into their study of the cosmos. The medievals at least owned up to theirs; perhaps it is time we do the same.

—⚹—

Though Lewis's space trilogy (*Out of the Silent Planet, Perelandra, That Hideous Strength*) was published several decades before *The Discarded Image,* it embodies thematically and geographically the full beauty, power, and majesty of the medieval model. To read these three novels is to be transported back to an older, more mystical conception of the cosmos, one where hierarchy, plenitude, and influence are still the rule. Thus, though Lewis adopts the modern ordering of the planets, he presents those planets as bastions of physical and spiritual life populated by rational creatures (or *hnau*) who live in unfallen, Edenic worlds of peace and plenty. Moreover, he explains (in *Out of the Silent Planet*) that each planet or sphere is watched over by a guardian spirit that he calls the *Oyarsa.* These Oyarsa, who are at once the archangels of the Bible and the intelligences of ancient astronomy, are both the servants of the Creator (Maleldil) and the masters of all those who live within their sphere. They bring order and harmony to their sphere, shedding over it and even radiating out into the cosmos their benign influence. Indeed, so great is their influence that it is felt on the earth, but not, the trilogy makes plain, in terms of some zodiacal determinism.

Rather, their influence is felt in the more essential, more humanistic realms of poetry, myth, and dreams. The Oyarsa are the true origins (the Platonic forms or Jungian archetypes, if you will) of all our deepest yearnings and most noble ideals. Thus, Lewis explains in the penultimate chapter of *Perelandra,* the Oyarsa of Mars (Malacandra) and Venus (Perelandra) are at once the guardian spirits of their planets and the final origin of those twin deities of war and love that the pagans worshiped. But his conception goes even deeper than that. When Lewis brings us face-to-face with these two ageless Oyarsa, he insists that what we are seeing is, in fact, the very essence of masculinity and femininity. The distinctions between the sexes are not, as modern feminists would have it, mere social and linguistic constructs, nor are they, as the secular scientists would have it, mere products of biology; they are, instead, earthly reflections of a celestial reality. That which, on our fallen, decaying, ever-changing world, retains only its mythic force is, in the perfect, unfallen world of the heavenly spheres, both historical and real. Indeed, Lewis informs us in chapter 13 of *That Hideous Strength* that King Arthur, whom medieval legend held was not dead but asleep on the isle of Avalon where he awaits the day when England shall need him again, dwells now on Perelandra (Venus) in company with those deathless prophets of the Old Testament, Enoch, Melchizedek, Moses, and Elijah. In an even more striking episode, Lewis climaxes *That Hideous Strength* by having the Oyarsa of all the planets descend to earth and shed their respective influences upon the forces of good in the novel, thereby empowering them to defeat their enemies.

However, it is not only in its wider spiritual and geographical dimensions that the space trilogy works as a fictional apologetic for our medieval past. More effective even than its celestial backdrop is the way Lewis allows us to experience the medieval model through the eyes of a modern protagonist who, like the Lewis of *Surprised by Joy,* progresses from a modern, scientific-minded, myth-exploding skeptic to a man of deep faith and humility whose eyes are permanently opened to greater spiritual realities. The story begins when Ransom, a philologist whose character is patterned partly on Lewis and partly on Tolkien, is kidnapped by two evil men and taken to Mars. From here, he quickly undergoes an "education" in the wonders of the unseen world, an education that begins when he looks out the window of the spaceship:

> He had read of "Space": at the back of his thinking for years had lurked the dismal fancy of the black, cold vacuity, the utter deadness, which was supposed to separate the worlds. He had not known how much it affected him till now—now that the very name "Space" seemed a blasphemous libel for this empyrean ocean of radiance in which they swam. . . . He had thought it barren: he saw now that it was the womb of worlds, whose blazing and innumerable offspring looked down nightly even upon the earth with so many eyes—and here, with how many more! No: Space was the wrong name. Older thinkers had been wiser when they named it simply the heavens . . . (*Out of the Silent Planet,* chapter 5)

The heavens, it seems, are far more wonderful than he had imagined.

In the second novel, Ransom, now apprised of the medieval model in all its glory, is carried by angels (the *eldila*) to Perelandra where he engages in a titanic struggle to prevent a demon-possessed man from tempting the innocent Queen of Venus. In the breathtaking closing chapter of that novel, Ransom, exhausted from his ordeal, is vouchsafed a sublime image of the final purpose and goal behind the spiritual battle he has waged on Venus and will (in *That Hideous Strength*) continue to wage on the earth. Like Dante in the final cantos of the *Divine Comedy,* Ransom's eyes are fully opened, and he glimpses the nature of paradise and the ultimate state of the blessed. For Dante, that image comes in the form of a Mystic Rose; for Lewis, who shares Dante's model, it comes in the form of a Great Dance. In both symbols, for that is finally what they are, the dominant image is one of perfect order fused with ceaseless interchange, a courtly pageant that is as stately and decorous as it is vital and joyous. As Lewis describes it, it is a hierarchical dance whose center ever shifts because its center is ever God, and whose participants get their turn at the center only because they remain within the hierarchy:

> Each figure as he looked at it became the master-
> figure or focus of the whole spectacle, by means of which
> his eye disentangled all else and brought it into unity—
> only itself to be entangled when he looked to what he
> had taken for mere marginal decorations and found that
> there also the same hegemony was claimed.

The beauty that lurks in perfect unity, the creativity that is discovered only in strict form, the freedom that comes only through surrender—all these things our modern world has forfeited. In the space trilogy, Lewis restores them to us in all their glory.

—ᴍ—

If the space trilogy carries the medieval model up into the heavens, then the Chronicles of Narnia bring it back to the earth. Lewis's concern in the latter series is not so much to contemplate the influence of the spheres or to uncover hidden angelic forces as it is to create a magical world in which nature is still alive and in sympathy with man. The fauns and dryads and talking horses that populate Narnia and its surrounding countries are more than just testaments to Lewis's wide reading in the annals of ancient myth and legend—they mark, as well, an attempt by Lewis to revive in his readers a sense of awe and wonder at the numinous presences that dwell all around us. What the reader often remembers about the Chronicles long after the plot details have faded is the intense vitality of Narnia; everything in that wondrous land seems to shimmer with life. Indeed, though the land of Narnia has been fervently embraced by orthodox Christians, it is much closer in conception to the kind of world the New Ager yearns to inhabit.

Aslan is, of course, an allegory for (or, better, a type of) Christ. Indeed, he *is* Christ in another form and by another name, as he intimates to the children on the final page of *The Voyage of the Dawn Treader,* but he is also the embodiment of Spring. In chapter 8 of *The Lion, the Witch and the Wardrobe,* Mr. Beaver shares the following prophetic poem with the children:

Wrong will be right, when Aslan comes in sight,

At the sound of his roar, sorrows will be no more,

When he bares his teeth, winter meets its death

And when he shakes his mane, we shall have spring again.

As we have already seen, Lewis firmly believed that in the person of Jesus Christ, both the prophecies of the Jews and the myths of the Greeks found their perfect and historical fulfillment. In constructing the character of Aslan, Lewis combined elements from both the Gospel narratives and the ancient pagan mysteries, particularly those celebrated at Eleusis. The salvation that Aslan effects in *The Lion, the Witch and the Wardrobe* is not just theological but natural. He ransoms both Edmund and Narnia from the White Witch, but he also brings fertility back to the land. This sympathetic relationship between the divine and the natural is, as we saw above, a vital aspect of the medieval model, as it is of the New Age, and, in the Chronicles, Lewis helps revive in his readers a sense both of the connectedness of all things and of the sacredness of the natural and the physical.

Lewis knew well the dangers that come with excessive Puritanism: denigration of the flesh, suspicion of the arts, and an abstract spirituality divorced from nature and from ritual. In the medieval Catholic world of Narnia, such things more naturally attach themselves to the White Witch, who hates all forms of revelry and of natural life. During the tyrannical reign of the Telmarines (*Prince Caspian*), not only is the natural world suppressed and rendered mute (transformed, Barfield might say, from a kindred subject to a dead object), but the tales of Aslan and the four kings are both forgotten and forbidden—an Enlightenment-type project that in our world would expunge not only the Gospel narratives but the romances of the Middle Ages. The Telmarines have not only rejected Aslan; they have rejected the joy and the magic that go with him. It is only appropriate then that when Aslan returns to reclaim Narnia both for himself (divine) and the talking animals (natural), he does so in tandem with Bacchus.

This scene has confused some of Lewis's readers. Why bring the Greek god of "wine, women, and song" into a nice Christian allegory for children? they ask, but the presence of Bacchus is fully consistent with the medieval conception of Lewis's series. First, the fusion of pagan and Christian was not, as we saw above, a problem for medievals like Dante, who took great joy and pride in their ability to synthesize and order vastly diverse elements. In true medieval fashion, Lewis incorporated into his Chronicles anything and everything that had ever given him a sense of the numinous, of that special awe that mingles beauty with fear—a sense he captures most fully in Shasta's meeting with Aslan in chapter 11 of *The Horse and His Boy*. This eclectic aspect of the Chronicles has bothered some of Lewis's critics (it particularly irked Tolkien the purist), but it is consistent with the medieval ethos. Second, to link Aslan to Bacchus is to make a point that those early Christians who chose December 25 to celebrate Christmas would have understood well—that though the Incarnation, Crucifixion, and Resurrection are real, historic events, they are also archetypal stories with great mythic force. Historically speaking, Christ is the Son of God, but he is also, mythically speaking, Bacchus, Balder, Osiris, Mithras, and the Corn King. Finally, Bacchus embodies life at its most ecstatic, that raw, earthy, bodily kind of life that shatters all hypocrisy and helps enable us to receive the fullness of life that Christ promises in John 10:10. It is a life that is also richness itself, enlivened by a desire to grow and develop, to break down barriers, to achieve our full, God-given potential.

Indeed, it is the same richness that is evident on the first day of Narnia's creation (*The Magician's Nephew*) when the power of Aslan's song is so strong that anything planted in the earth—from a piece of candy to a bit of a lamppost—will grow. Unfortunately, the evil characters in *The Magician's Nephew* (Uncle Andrew and Queen Jadis) are unable to see or hear the beauty of Aslan's song, for, like the Telmarines and the dwarves in the stable at the end of *The Last Battle,* they are afraid of life, hate joy, and mistrust magic. Similarly, we moderns do not see in the heavens the life, joy, and magic that the medievals did, not because it is not there, but because we simply refuse to see it. Again, we have eyes but do not see, ears but do not hear. Of course, we *could* see and hear again, but to do that, we would first have to revive in our minds the power and beauty of the medieval model, and second, become in our hearts like children again. To read the Chronicles of Narnia as a modern adult is to be empowered to do both at once.

The Chronicles at their most effective allow us to see our own world afresh, and, by so doing, to gain some needed humility. When reformed "brat" Eustace Scrubb learns (in *Voyage of the Dawn Treader,* chapter 14) that Ramandu the magician is actually a retired star, he exclaims that on earth, stars are only huge balls of flaming gas. Ramandu's answer is at once a slight reprimand to the overeager Eustace and a not-so-slight rebuke to all moderns who think they can reduce to abstract laws the glories of the heavens: "'Even in your world, my son, that is not what a star is but only what it is made of.'"

—⁓—

If we are to effectively meet the challenge of the New Age, then we must, like Lewis, find ways to re-embody, indeed, "reincarnate" the sympathetic universe and the inclusivist vision that mark the medieval model at its most exalted. Of course, part of the Enlightenment-Reformation propaganda leveled against the Medieval Church would have us believe that the medievals were rigid, inflexible heresy-hunters (after the flat earth, the Spanish Inquisition is what comes first to most minds when thinking of the Middle Ages). And yet, is it not our own era that has proven most relentless in its quest for scientific, social, political, and doctrinal purity?

Our message, if it is to ring true with the New Ager, must be that of Emeth in the final book of the Chronicles, *The Last Battle.* Emeth is a Calormene from the South and a member of a religion that does not worship Aslan. And yet, when Emeth dies at the end of the novel, he is not cast into utter darkness with the others who do not know Aslan but finds himself in a grassy meadow bathed in sunlight. He goes in search of Tash, the pagan god he has worshiped piously all his life, but does not find him. Rather, he is met (in chapter 15) by Aslan, who explains to the noble Calormene that all the good he has done in the name of Tash has been accounted as good to Aslan. Emeth is afraid, but "by reason of [his] great desire for wisdom and understanding" he approaches and questions the Lion. Constrained to tell the truth, he confesses that it was Tash and not Aslan he had sought all his life. But Aslan replies gently, "Beloved, . . . unless thy desire had been for me thou wouldst not have sought so long and so truly. For all find what they truly seek." Like the Magi of old, faith and salvation in Aslan marks for Emeth the end of a long spiritual pilgrimage.

If we interpret the story of Emeth as a defense of universal salvation, then we will misunderstand both Lewis and his medieval vision. Had Emeth rejected Aslan and clung still to Tash, he would have been cast out of the Narnian heaven. But he does not reject Aslan, for he recognizes in him (as the Magi, Cornelius, and the Samaritan woman recognized in Christ) the true object and end of his lifelong search. Though his journey round and up the hill has been a circuitous one, at the top of that hill he finds his heart's desire and is embraced by the velveted paws of Aslan.

May all those in the New Age who share that desire find him, our Aslan and our Christ, as well, and may we in the church learn to facilitate their journey. Amen and amen.

4

Wrestling with Evil
and Suffering

The Problem of Pain

There are many reasons why people reject religion in general and Christianity in particular, but the one that strikes deepest—the one that stabs at the gut and that leads first to anger and then to apathy—is the one that brings us back irresistibly to that age-old question: If God is so good, then why is there so much evil and suffering in the world? Prick under the surface of the majority of unbelievers, especially those who have consciously distanced themselves from an early, simplistic faith, and you will discover a simmering hostility, only slightly suppressed, at all those "sweetness and light" phrases that Christians like to use: God is love; God is in control; All things work together for good; Only God knows what is best for us. Such people should not be ridiculed or taken lightly. The root of their anger is generally real and almost always sincere. Like the young C. S. Lewis, they may have experienced some great pain or loss or disappointment in their lives, a moment of tragedy which they fervently but unsuccessfully prayed would pass over them. They may have stared into the darkness above and felt abandoned and impotent in the face of a universe which they now see as uncaring and impersonal. The experience is a common one that cuts across time, race, sex, and culture, and it has led many a person to resist or abandon any real faith in a personal and loving God.

This much is well known and has often been discussed. What is less often asked is why our modern Western world, which has seen a decrease in human suffering unparalleled in human history, seems less able to deal with pain and more quick either to blame God for evil and suffering or to deny his existence altogether—or, as contradictory as it may seem, to do both at the same time. We seem to have lost our ability to adequately wrestle with this most persistent of problems; instead, with each decade that passes, we grow more and more angry with God, even as we believe in him less and less.

At the root of our modern, post-Enlightenment inability (or at least, unwillingness) to deal with evil and suffering lies a radical change in our view of ourselves, our potential, and what it is that prevents us from fulfilling that potential. The change begins in the eighteenth century with the writings of one of the shapers of the modern world, Jean Jacques Rousseau (1712–1778). In traditional Christian thought, the problem with humanity is sin: lust, pride, and disobedience. Though we are made in God's image and thus capable of great things, all that we do is marred by our inner rebellion against God. But for Rousseau and those who have followed in his footsteps, the real problem is not sin but ignorance, not pride but poverty. The sickness that eats away at our potential greatness is not so much spiritual as it is societal. In the state of nature, Rousseau argued, we are free and good, but society corrupts us. Purify society, clean out the systemic evil, improve our physical conditions; then, and only then, will men sprout wings and halos.

Buoyed up by Rousseau's faith in the perfectibility of man, a faith that lies at the core of modern liberal thought, the great reformers of the late eighteenth and nineteenth centuries set out to build a utopia in which ignorance, greed, and poverty would be eradicated. This liberal, utopian dream reached its apex during the Victorian Age, when philosophers and writers such as John Stuart Mill, Alfred, Lord Tennyson, and H. G. Wells argued forcefully and dreamed magnificently that mankind, through the benefits of science, technology, and social planning would propel itself into a millennial kingdom of universal peace and brotherhood. At first, this faith was essentially theistic in outlook, but as the nineteenth century wore on, it came to influence even nonreligious thinkers like Marx, who believed that history was moving unstoppably toward a utopia of pure communism. In its former incarnation (which includes the European Union as well as the ongoing American "experiment" from the Constitution to the Great Society), this faith has proven relatively benign. In its latter incarnation, however (which includes the utopian dreams of Robespierre, Stalin, Hitler, and Castro), it has proven deadly. All four of these tyrants (and those like them) fancied that they could construct a new kind of community (and a new kind of human) that would mark the end point and culmination of the long human struggle. Unfortunately, to accomplish this goal they would have to eradicate from their brave new states all traces of that societal corruption that they saw as the prime obstacle to achieving their goal. The source of that corruption constantly shifts, from aristocrats to bourgeois farmers, Jews to capitalists, but what does not shift is the destructive belief that if that specific corruption can be successfully removed, mankind will enter utopia. Had these tyrants accepted that the problem with humanity was sin, they would have seen the mad impossibility of their schemes, for evil does not rest in one particular group or in a specific social malady, but in the heart of every fallen human being. But precisely *because* they believed the human was perfectible, they were willing to go to any lengths, including murder, injustice, and genocide, to effect that perfectibility.

It is really one of history's most terrible ironies. The supposedly "optimistic" view of man that begins with Rousseau leads to a long list of totalitarian, antihumanistic states that crush all individuality and purge out all difference—a nightmare that C. S. Lewis prophesied in *The Abolition of Man* and fictionalized in *That Hideous Strength.* And it is an irony that was propounded further by a paradox. The liberal tradition claims to champion humanity's unlimited potential and to affirm the freedom of its will and of its power to choose; yet, in the thought of many of the most influential modernists (Darwin, Freud, Marx, and others), there runs a very strong vein of determinism, whether it be biological, psychological, historical, or political. Mankind is both freer and more enslaved than it ever was in the days when the Christian view that man is made in God's image but fallen prevailed throughout Europe. The solution to the paradox is not hard to locate. Once humans ceased to be measured against God and began to be measured against nature, they both gained and lost in the transaction. Freed from any final accountability to the moral standards of a holy God, humanity seemed poised to grow into a glorious creature of its own making. This freedom, however, was bought at a price: that of reducing the human race to the status of the animal world and thus placing it under the sway of natural processes that run apart from human will and desires and that are as impersonal as they are inexorable. The totalitarian dark side of nineteenth-century liberal optimism produced nations and governments whose leaders saw themselves as the force of history itself and who saw humanity as a thing to be molded by evolutionary forces that they themselves controlled.

Yet still, despite the horrors of totalitarianism from both the right and the left, Westerners continue to cherish the dream of utopia and the one-world government. Political economist Francis Fukuyama predicted in the early 1990s that all of history was moving toward an almost universal acceptance of liberal democracy, and his prophecy continues to hold mostly true even in the face of the terrible events of September 11, 2001. Indeed, the rise of global terrorism may, in the end, provide us all with a clear center and cause of corruption and thus, ironically, keep alive the liberal dream of our perfectibility this side of heaven. The modern Western citizen still thinks we can build a heaven on earth, that we can stave off death, that we can control and manipulate both the outer environment (nature) and the "inner environment" (the propensity for lust, greed, and violence). In the face of a century of totalitarian nightmares, mankind continues to cherish those utopian dreams.

—⁓—

I have now digressed long and deeply on a subject that may at first seem totally unrelated to the thesis of this chapter, that of the modern era's feeble and inadequate response to evil and suffering. But I really have not. For at the core of our inability to wrestle with the problem of pain lies our misunderstanding of who we are as fallen creatures made in the image of God. Because we misunderstand the first part—that we are fallen, we imagine that we can eradicate all evil and suffering and are shocked and disappointed when we fail to do so. Because we misunderstand the second part, that we are made in God's image, we slip into a biological and environmental determinism that abdicates us from responsibility for our actions and leaves us feeling victimized when things go wrong. Ironically, though both cases leave God out of the equation, when failure results and suffering ensues we tend to put the blame on God. We do this in the former case because he did not "bail us out"; in the latter because he "made us that way."

Our modern experiments in utopia and the perfection of mankind have instilled in us a this-worldly view of ourselves and our destiny that posits the pursuit of happiness as an inalienable right and that defines that happiness as the maximization of pleasure and the minimization of pain. Now there is no question that liberal democracy and free market capitalism have proven great boons for the human race and that advances in science and technology have made our lives easier, better, and more healthy. Unfortunately, we have allowed these praiseworthy accomplishments to cloud the issue of why we were created and what our true purpose is. As a result, we have failed to understand the necessity, cause, and purpose of pain. We have constructed a user-friendly God whom we can ignore or render irrelevant when things go well and against whom we can rage when things go wrong. Either that, or as totalitarian states are most adept at doing, we have reduced God to the force of destiny or the process of evolution. Unfortunately, when God is so reduced, a deterministic mind-set ensues that obscures the question of why there is evil in the world. As a result, we have failed to understand the full nature and ultimate origin of human depravity.

As Lewis succinctly describes it in the second chapter of *The Problem of Pain,* the great insoluble riddle that is posed by the evil and suffering in our world is simply this: How can God be both all-loving and all-powerful and yet allow pain? Indeed, the fact that evil and suffering exist suggests that he is either not loving enough to desire, or not powerful enough to accomplish, their elimination. Philosophers and theologians who struggle with this riddle refer to it as a *theodicy*: a meditation on God's justice. The book of Job is a theodicy, for it seeks to uncover a cause and a purpose for Job's seemingly unmerited suffering. Habakkuk is also a theodicy, one that asks a related question: Why do the ways of sinners prosper? Milton's *Paradise Lost* is an epic theodicy that seeks "to justify the ways of God to man."

What is the origin of evil? Why is there death in our world? What is the cause/effect purpose behind pain and suffering? How can an event like the Holocaust or the 9/11 attack on the World Trade Center occur in a world created and run by a loving and compassionate God? These are the questions that a theodicy seeks to answer, questions that our liberal belief in man's innate goodness and our modernist-paradigm based acceptance of biological and environmental determinism have left us powerless to answer.

But Lewis Agonistes, precisely because he was unafraid to wrestle with both of these tenets of the modern liberal world, was also able to come closer to a solution (or at least an understanding, since no real solution exists this side of the grave) to the perennial and often faith-destroying problem of pain.

God's Free Will Experiment

In the previous two chapters, we seconded Lewis Agonistes as he mounted first a reactive defense that took him back to an older, medieval solution to the challenge at hand, and then followed with a proactive offense in which he sought to forge a new vision out of the raw material of traditional Christendom. In this chapter I shall follow a somewhat different organization, one that befits more the particular struggle under consideration. Here the opposing motions shall not be backward and forward, but general and specific, abstract and personal. Thus, we shall first explore how Lewis in *The Problem of Pain* revived the parameters of traditional Christian theodicy and recast them in a fresh, genial, modern way. Then, having expounded Lewis's intellectual answer to evil and suffering, we shall turn to *A Grief Observed* and witness his slow and agonizing attempt to readdress the problem of pain, not for readers seeking a theological solution, but as a way to reconcile his own inner pain, loss, and doubt.

If we are to address the origin and purpose of evil and suffering, Lewis argues in *The Problem of Pain,* we must understand and come to grips with three things: the nature of God's free will experiment, our status as fallen creatures, and the obstacle that prevents us from achieving our full potential. Lewis devotes chapters 2 and 3 to exploring the first, chapters 4 and 5 to exploring the second, and chapters 6 and 7 to exploring the third. In all three sections, he borrows heavily from the writings of the fathers of the church, while adding always a modern twist that challenges those of us living in a liberal, post-Enlightenment world to rethink our accepted views of ourselves and our choices.

First, it must be understood that Lewis's theodicy is a free will theodicy with the courage of its convictions. Lewis will not allow us to play any theological games in which we argue that God gave us free will and simultaneously withheld it. To say that God did both at the same time is nonsense, and "nonsense," Lewis reminds us at the start of chapter 2, "remains nonsense even when we talk it about God." Lewis rejects immediately the modern penchant for determinism both in its materialist and its Christian (i.e., hyper-Calvinist) forms. If God has predestined all our actions from the beginning, then free will is nothing but a charade. And if it is nothing but a charade, then at least two things follow. First, man is not really a creature made in the image of God, since this phrase can mean nothing if it does not include consciousness, rationality, and volition—the three are, indeed, inseparable. Second, if our will is not free and our choices are not our own, then we must, in one way or another, lay the charge for the origin of evil on the shoulders of God. Evil arises from a misuse of free will both in the angelic and human spheres that causes what God created in a state of goodness to be corrupted and perverted. But if we had no choice but to fall, if it was forced upon us from above, then God ultimately must take the blame. This is not to deny the Catholic concept of the *felix culpa* (or blessed guilt), which considers the Fall of Adam and Eve to be a good event because it led to God's greater outpouring of love in the person of Christ. Just because God is in the business of redeeming that which we humans have destroyed, let us not, therefore, think that he initiated the destruction so that he might have the satisfaction of cleaning up the mess.

Lewis's rejection of predestination also does not imply that he believed (as some Openness theologians have begun to believe) that God's knowledge of the future is limited. Lewis accepted fully that God knows the future, but he refused to make a link, as so many Christians have done, between divine foreknowledge and predestination. Again and again in his work (most notably in book 4, chapter 3 of *Mere Christianity*), Lewis argues convincingly that most people do not understand what the Bible means when it says that God knows the future. Yes, from our limited, time-enslaved, human point of view, foreknowledge *does* necessitate predestination, but God lives outside of time and space in a realm where all is eternally present. God does not, technically speaking, foresee the future. Indeed, he does not foresee anything. To foresee suggests that the viewer is locked into a temporal system of past, present, and future. God does not *foresee* the future; he *sees* it in the same way that we see the present. If we accept this vital distinction, an interesting proposition emerges: if my seeing of a present event does not determine it, why should God's eternally present seeing of a future event that is, future to us—determine its outcome? Or, to put it another way, since God's knowledge is ever and always a *present* knowledge of our *present* choice, our freedom is not violated.

Here, then, is where we must begin, with an unshakable and unqualified assertion that God of his own free will chose to endow his human creatures with the power of choice. Indeed, if it is not blasphemous to express it this way, God's creation of the human race represents, in part, a free will experiment. God chose, for reasons he did not choose to share with us, to make us volitional creatures, and, by so doing, he left himself open to the consequences that accompany such a decision. You see, most Christians would agree with Lewis that God gave us free will, but few have ever considered what exactly is involved in such a monumental decision. Choice, though it rises up from within the individual, is a thing that can only exist fully within a community of other choice-making individuals. If God had created us as a scattered mass of bodiless spirits flitting around in the infinite reaches of space, then his free will experiment would have been rendered null and void from the start. To ensure real and meaningful choice there must be both interaction and resistance, and to ensure these necessary activities, we must have bodies, or at least something like bodies, that can interact and resist.

But bodies, too, are not enough. For each of these ensouled bodies to act out its free will, there must be an arena, a stage, a neutral playing field against which all of these various choices can be enacted. Furthermore, that field, if it is to perform its role, must be fixed and stable: something like the natural, physical world in which we live. Were it not fixed and could I as an individual constantly reshape it in accordance with my own desires, then, once again, the free will experiment would be jeopardized. For each time I changed the playing field, I would be robbing others of their free will. Nature, therefore, must be fixed, but a nature that is fixed is also one that is unyielding, one that can cause pain and suffering if it is collided with. Some might ask why God does not then intervene to soften the impact with nature—to cause a rock, say, to turn into a sponge so we will not be injured when we fall on it. Well, in some instances, God does just that when he performs a miracle, but if God were to intervene every time someone was in danger, then nature would quickly lose its "fixedness," and the whole free will proposition would come crashing down. Though one can occasionally bend the rules of a game, if one throws out the rules or renders all of them arbitrary and amendable, then the game, *as* a game, will simply cease to exist. This may not be, Lewis concludes, the best of all possible worlds, but it just may be the only possible *kind* of world that God could have created to facilitate the game he wished to play. A modicum of pain, or at least the possibility of pain, seems to have been written into the very script of our planet and to have existed even in the prelapsarian world of the Garden of Eden.

A major part of the liberal, utopian dream, as we saw above, consists in freeing humanity from all dependence on nature. In some senses, this is a noble goal, but it is also one that is finally antihuman. For part of our definition as volitional beings who must actively shape themselves against a resistant playing field rests on the fixed intransigence of nature. But there is a deeper problem with the utopian dream. As noted earlier, the goal of the post-Enlightenment reformer is twofold: to maximize pleasure and minimize pain; to safeguard the pursuit of happiness. Again, these goals in and of themselves are noble ones, but they hide from us the very purpose of God's free will experiment. God did not place us on this terrestrial stage merely to have fun; he placed us here to grow and develop through the proper exercising and surrendering of our wills into the creatures he created us to be. We claim to want and to worship a Father in heaven, writes Lewis in chapter 3, but what we really want is "a grandfather in heaven—a senile benevolence who, as they say, 'liked to see young people enjoying themselves,' and whose plan for the universe was simply that it might be truly said at the end of each day, 'a good time was had by all.'" The love of God that impelled him to give us free will is not the indulgent love of a grandfather who just wants to see us smile, but the tough love of a father who is willing to do what it takes to shape his sons and daughters into persons of integrity.

Though a good father wishes to see his son happy, he would rather see him unsuccessful but virtuous than prosperous but unjust. God loves us, and, as such, he "labour[s] to make us lovable," even if the process by which that birthing occurs involves some pain and suffering. There are times in our lives when we wish for God to leave us alone, but to ask God to stop "meddling" with us is to ask him to stop loving us. It is to ask the artist to cease working on his potential masterpiece. We (like God) only discipline those whom we love.

> It is for people whom we care nothing about that we demand happiness on any terms: with our friends, our lovers, our children, we are exacting and would rather see them suffer much than be happy in contemptible and estranging modes. If God is Love, He is, by definition, something more than mere kindness. And it appears, from all the records, that though He has often rebuked us and condemned us, He has never regarded us with

contempt. He has paid us the intolerable compliment of
loving us, in the deepest, most tragic, most inexorable
sense. (*The Problem of Pain*, chapter 3)

If our world is a game, it is a very serious one: one whose stakes are
so high that even suffering (even onto the loss of an eye or a hand) is
counted no great loss if it enables us to grow into sons worthy of the
divine Father who made us.

But of course, the degree of pain that would call for an eye or a
hand—the degree of pain, that is, that we encounter daily in our world—
was not part of the original plan. Evil and suffering as we know it is the
result of the Fall, not of the free will experiment that made possible that
Fall. And so, if we are truly to understand the problem of pain, then we
must understand exactly what was involved in the Fall. This Lewis does
for us, but in a way that is wholly unique to him. I argued in my first
chapter that Lewis, in his life and his apologetics, combined reason with
intuition, logic with imagination. Nowhere is this more evident than in
the fourth and fifth chapters of *The Problem of Pain*, chapters that Lewis
devotes to the spinning of an elaborate myth of creation, temptation,
and fall.

By "myth," Lewis informs us in a note, he does not mean "a sym-
bolical representation of a non-historical truth," but "an account of what
may have been the historical fact." In other words, using Genesis 1–3 as
his guide, Lewis attempts to fashion a narrative to explain the nature of
our original state of innocence and how and why we lost that innocence.
In the myth that Lewis conjures for us, God makes use of natural
processes to slowly evolve our body into its present form. At some point
in this process, however, God intervenes directly to breathe into us our
soul. Before that point, we were simply physical creatures with no consciousness of our own existence. But once our body is fused with a God-
breathed spirit, we become a living soul (an "I") with the power to make
judgments, to perceive beauty, and to know God in an intimate, rela-
tional way. While in this primal state, all is unified and effortless. Our
soul directs our body, and our mind is free from any type of phobia or
neurosis that would stifle or misdirect it. The kind of control that the
Hindu mystic claims to hold over his voluntary and involuntary muscles

is ours in full; we are the masters of our emotions, our desires, and our instincts. The animals recognize us as their natural lords and pay us homage, even as we care for them and draw out their potential. And yet, despite our lordship over the animals and despite the fact that we have a full sense of ourselves as individual beings, we gracefully surrender ourselves and our wills to our Creator. Obedience comes to us naturally, and we take great joy in yielding to the loving commands of the Father. The surrender *does* call for a slight bowing of the will, but it is a pleasant surrender, not unlike those thousand little concessions that honeymoon lovers are happy and eager to make to each other.

In his novel *Perelandra,* written three years after *The Problem of Pain,* Lewis expands his myth to a near epic scale. On the wings of soaring prose, Lewis spirits us away to the planet Venus, where we are introduced to its lovely, unfallen Queen. The Queen (or Lady) carries on an uninterrupted dialogue with her Creator Maleldil, who speaks to her telepathically in a direct and intimate way. As he speaks, she submits happily to his will, and as she submits, she learns and grows. Maleldil has given all things to the Lady and her mate the King, but like the God of Genesis, he has forbidden them one thing. Much of Perelandra is covered with water, and over those waters, great floating islands move and fluctuate with the tide. Though Maleldil allows the King and Queen to walk by day on fixed land, he commands them to spend their nights on the floating islands.

Lewis, of course, means this strange command issued by Maleldil the Creator to parallel God's command against the eating of the fruit of the knowledge of good and of evil. It is partly Lewis's way of instructing his reader that the Fall of Adam and Eve had less to do with the eating of a magic fruit than it did with disobedience. (Lewis offers a similar insight in his most lasting and accessible academic work, *A Preface to "Paradise Lost,"* which he wrote in the three-year interim that separates *The Problem of Pain* from *Perelandra.*) In eating the "apple," Adam and Eve rebelled against the authority of God; similarly, had the King and Queen of Venus forsaken Maleldil's command and slept on fixed land, they would have shown themselves unwilling to abide by the laws of their Creator. However, Lewis does something far more subtle with his fixed-land command than merely parallel the fruit of knowledge. Indeed, by means of this command, Lewis helps identify for the reader the specific *nature* of that disobedience which caused us to lose Paradise.

At the root of spiritual disobedience is the desire to call ourselves our own: to cease being adjectives for the glory of God and to seek, instead, to be our own self-sufficient nouns. Were the Lady to sleep on fixed land, she would be, in effect, seeking a kind of stability that Maleldil did not desire for her to have. Though everything on Perelandra belongs to the Lady, she does not actually possess anything. She receives all things daily from Maleldil and is burdened by no craving for private property. She experiences every possible kind of pleasure, but she does not lust to own that pleasure. She resists what Lewis calls the temptation for an "encore": the desire to possess a thrill and to hold it forever at our beck and call. She is content to remain a sojourner on the floating islands of Perelandra, and will not attempt to carve out for herself a piece of land that is hers and hers alone. She accepts that her highest end, if I may paraphrase the Westminster Shorter Catechism, is to glorify Maleldil and enjoy him forever.

Unfortunately, the terrestrial Adam and Eve proved less obedient and less willing to forgo the encore than the King and Queen of Venus. Unlike the Lady, we selfishly chose to call our soul our own, and to return to Lewis's myth in *The Problem of Pain,* our choice led to a devastating result—our loss of status as a species. Having rejected God's higher laws, we immediately fell prey to the lower laws of nature originally created to control the animals. Our soul ceased to be the lord of our body and became its prisoner instead. As a result, our body fell sway to base and destructive appetites and to the suffering and pain that naturally ensue when our lusts are given the upper hand. Even our mind, once free of all phobias, fell sway to material, psychological forces. Without the soul to guide it, our body waxed rebellious and thus opened itself to natural decay. Our mind, on the other hand, unable to handle its own lusts and those of the body, began a long and tortured process of repression and denial which, in time, formed the unconscious mind.

In the end, mankind emerged as a mere shadow of what it once had been. Indeed, in a sad but real sense, humans were no longer the creatures that God had created them to be. "A new species," writes Lewis, "never made by God, had sinned itself into existence." Along with this new species, came a new, fallen nature and, with it, a new kind and degree of pain never known—never intended to be known—in the Garden of Eden. We say that evil and suffering are a result of the Fall, and we are right in saying so. What we do not realize when we make this statement, however, is that evil and suffering are not so much a punishment for disobedience as they are the natural outgrowth of our decision to call our souls our own. When we refused to live in direct communion with and full reliance upon the One who created us—when we chose to go our own way and to amass our own private happiness—we catapulted ourselves out of the eternal richness and harmony of the Garden and into a fragmented world of disharmony and decay in which time is always running down. Or, to paraphrase St. Paul, we subjected ourselves and our world to futility. The delicate balance of mind, body, and soul within and of the natural cycles without have been disrupted by our fatal, rebellious grasp at an unnatural and unintended self-sufficiency. The upshot has been, on the one hand, corruption and perversion, which are the origins of evil, and, on the other, entropy and disease, which are the origins of suffering.

—⁓—

Pain, then, is an unintended consequence of our primal disobedience. But that is not the whole story. Just as God redeemed the Fall (*felix culpa*) and made it the vehicle for the loving sacrifice and victorious resurrection of his Son, so God has so redeemed pain as to make it a tool for calling us back to obedience. For, despite the Fall, we are still called to obedience, and, though our fallen nature prevents us from achieving it apart from the grace of Christ, we are yet aware of the difference between good and evil, right and wrong. Just as Lewis rejects any hyper-Calvinistic notion of predestination, so does he reject as well the doctrine of total depravity. "I disbelieve that doctrine," he writes in chapter 4, "partly on the logical ground that if our depravity were total we should not know ourselves to be depraved, and partly because experience shows us much goodness in human nature." Though fallen, the human race nevertheless retains the image of God, and, with it, the power to choose, to judge, and to discern. And, though these powers have all been tainted by sin, they have not been revoked or rendered completely inert. The fact is that we still retain the knowledge that our proper good is to surrender to our Creator, even as we continue to refuse to offer that surrender.

Perhaps the most devastating result of the Fall is that the process of submitting to God, which was a pleasant and easy one in the Garden, has become hard, bitter, and painful. Rousseau was wrong; what holds us back from utopia is not ignorance. We know very well the righteousness that is expected of us, but our sin and pride cause us to resist the call of God. We are like willful children who simply will not give in. All of us, male and female, child and adult, are possessed of what Lewis calls in chapter 6 "the black, Satanic wish to kill or die rather than give in." That wish manifests itself in a thousand different ways, from the tyrant who ruthlessly executes his opponents to the child who breaks his toys so his siblings will not be able to play with them.

If God is to reach us and to lead us back to our original condition and beyond, he must break through this wall of resistance. If he is to teach us again that he alone is our refuge and that in him only can we find peace, joy, and purpose, then he must find some way to tear down those self-protective houses that we all build around ourselves. But how is God's call to be heard over the din of our inflated and clamorous egos? Here is where pain enters the equation: "God whispers to us in our pleasures, speaks in our conscience, but shouts in our pains: it is His megaphone to rouse a deaf world." For many of us, only the crushing experience of pain can force us to stop and examine ourselves. Only when we are confronted with suffering do we question our long and firmly held belief in our own self-sufficiency. Pain topples our house of cards: not once, but again and again. For we are such creatures that no sooner do we learn the lesson of the toppled cards, then we begin to build the house again.

Pain then is, at times, the natural consequence of our primal rebellion and, at others, a tool used by God to shatter our self-sufficiency. Unfortunately, it is not for us as fallen creatures possessed of limited understanding to say with certainty when the former is being played out and when the latter. It is enough that we know that suffering, though it is not good in itself, can be used for redemptive purposes, and that, given the fallen state of our world, our acts of submission and surrender are bound to be accompanied by some form of pain.

We may also take consolation in three aspects of pain that Lewis discusses in chapter 7. First, we can stop deluding ourselves with liberal promises of utopia and accept the fact that evil and suffering shall never be eradicated until Christ returns and establishes his kingdom. By so doing, we will not set ourselves up for continual disappointment. If we can remember that, in the words of an old hymn, "this world is not our home," then we will be better prepared for tragedy when it comes and more appreciative of joy while it lasts. Second, we can stop torturing ourselves with horrible thoughts about the terrible sum of human misery on our planet today. There is no such thing, Lewis reminds us, as a *sum* of human misery. "When we have reached the maximum that a single person can suffer, . . . we have reached all the suffering that there ever can be in the universe. The addition of a million fellow-sufferers adds no more pain." Finally, we can take solace in the fact that unlike spiritual evil, which corrupts all that it touches, physical pain is a "disinfected" kind of evil that leaves no lasting scars on its victims. Once the pain is ended, it is ended. Our modern world, with its fear of pain and its avoidance of death, has made suffering into a much darker and more poisonous creature than it is. Pain, like death, holds no power over those who pass through it and emerge safely on the other side.

When all is said and done, Lewis leaves us at the end of chapter 7 with an image of our world that we would do well to absorb into our psyche:

> The Christian doctrine of suffering explains,
> I believe, a very curious fact about the world we live in.
> The settled happiness and security which we all desire,
> God withholds from us by the very nature of the world:

but joy, pleasure, and merriment He has scattered broadcast. We are never safe, but we have plenty of fun and some ecstasy. It is not hard to see why. The security we crave would teach us to rest our hearts in this world and oppose an obstacle to our return to God: a few moments of happy love, a landscape, a symphony, a merry meeting with our friends, a bathe or a football match, have no such tendency. Our Father refreshes us on the journey with some pleasant inns, but will not encourage us to mistake them for home.

Indeed, this world is not our home, but it is also not simply a vale of tears. It is but a stage on a journey, but it is an important one, to be invested in with vigor. We are, in a sense, like Chaucer's pilgrims making their way to Canterbury. The destination is the purpose of the journey—without that destination the journey would be a meaningless one—but, as long as we keep our focus on that destination, there is no reason why we can't make merry and tell good tales on the way.

Suffering into Wisdom

Twenty years after writing *The Problem of Pain*, C. S. Lewis would find himself in a personal situation where the grief and pain of loss would threaten to tear down his own apologetical house of cards. I have already documented in the concluding section of chapter 1 how Lewis, a bachelor well into his fifties, married Joy Davidman Gresham, only to lose her three years later to cancer. I discussed there, as well, how Lewis dealt with his grief by keeping a journal that he later published as *A Grief Observed*. Here I shall concentrate instead on the slow and painful process by which Lewis pulled himself out of despair into a renewed and reinvigorated faith. There have been a few Lewis critics, most notably, John Beversluis and A. N. Wilson, who have attempted to wield *A Grief Observed* as a weapon for demolishing Lewis's earlier apologetics—"Mr. Know-it-all gets his comeuppance" is the underlying theme of their approach. Aside from the sheer vulgarity and tastelessness of their unfounded critique, it demonstrates a misunderstanding of Lewis and his works. *A Grief Observed* is in no way a refutation of Lewis's firm belief that Christian doctrine is logically and rationally sound; it presents us rather with the inner struggles of an apologist who finds that he must relearn and reexperience what he believes from a new vantage point. It is the memoir of a wounded soul temporarily stripped of its logic and rationality and forced to wrestle it out in a new, seemingly barren, arena.

Indeed, one need only read the first few pages of *A Grief Observed* to realize that the cool logic and carefully reasoned arguments of *The Problem of Pain* are very far away. Lewis is hurt, confused, and afraid, and he cries out in despair: Why, O Lord, did you pull me out of my safe, peaceful bachelorhood only to thrust me back once again into my shell? Why didn't you just leave me where I was? Why did you open my heart to a new kind of joy and then just as quickly rip that joy away? The following paraphrase of Lewis's lines offers a summary of his anguished musings:

> None of it makes sense. My marriage to Joy did not
> take me away from God. To the contrary, her mind
> sharpened my own and helped make me a fuller
> Christian. But now she is gone, and our marriage
> threatens to fade from memory, to be reduced to a brief,
> charming episode with no substance or lasting value. My
> Lord, I cannot even remember what her face looked like.
> How weary, stale, flat, and unprofitable everything
> seems; it is all dead and gray. Yes, she is now immortal
> and with God, but what good does that do me? I am
> isolated, alone, and cut off, like an amputee who must
> now try to balance himself on a single leg.
>
> And where is God? When I was happy and did not
> need him, his presence lay thick around me. But now,
> when I most desperately need him, when I cry out for
> him in my pain and grief, I only hear a door slamming
> in my face "and a sound of bolting and double bolting.
> After that, silence." No, I cannot cease believing in God;
> I might just as well stop believing in my own existence.
> But what kind of a God is he? Perhaps he is not a good

and loving God. Perhaps he is a Cosmic Sadist, an
Eternal Vivisector.

In time, the answers come, but they do not come logically or
systematically, as they do in *The Problem of Pain*. They come, rather, in a
tentative, fragmented form, slowly, painfully, and anecdotally.

I accuse God of being a vivisector, but to a sick
animal would not the kindest veterinarian seem as such?
Perhaps God, like a doctor, must often hurt to heal?
Besides, did not Jesus promise us that there would be
pain and grief in our world?

I accuse God of slamming the door, but perhaps it
was I who slammed the door in *his* face. If a drowning
man clutches too strongly and desperately to the
swimmer who is trying to save him, then he cannot be
rescued. Instead, he will drag both himself and his
rescuer under the waves. Yes, God invited us to knock on
the door, but surely not to bang on it.

No, my grief is not an end, not a fall into darkness.
It is a process, another movement in that dance of
creation, fall, and redemption that is older than time.
I must learn to live through this phase just as I have lived
through the others.

I say that my marriage to Joy did not take me away
from God, but is that fully true? Was it Joy that I loved,
or only my image of her? Did God have to shatter that
image lest I turn it into an idol? Even now, as I call out to
God in my grief, am I really seeking God himself or only
seeking to use him as a vehicle for getting Joy back? God
and heaven must be sought as ends-in-themselves, not
merely as a means for being reunited with Joy. How
often has God had to topple my house of cards? Perhaps
he had to destroy my image of Joy lest I make her into an
idol that would block me from him? God is, after all, the
greatest of iconoclasts. He must shatter even our ideas of

him, lest we worship the idea and not him who is the origin of the idea.

I cry that I cannot remember Joy's face, that I cannot conjure it up in my mind's eye. But that is because I sought it too hard. When I let go of my grief, when I stopped trying to hold on to that joy (and Joy) that I never really possessed, the image of her face came flooding back into my mind. And with it a mystical touch, a sense that she is part of a society of pure intelligence.

And I glimpsed as well something of God's great experiment. "Or no; not an experiment, for you have no need to find things out. Rather your grand enterprise. To make an organism which is also a spirit; to make that terrible oxymoron, a 'spiritual animal.' To take a poor primate, a beast with nerve-endings all over it, a creature with a stomach that wants to be filled, a breeding animal that wants its mate, and say, 'Now get on with it. Become a god.'" Christ became like us, so that we, someday, might become like him. We are gods in the making. Had we not sinned in the Garden, had we not chosen to call our soul our own, that transition into god-likeness would have been an easy one. But now it is accompanied by pain: the pain of death which is also the pain of birth.

And then there came that vision that allowed me, at last, to understand the true nature of my situation. "Imagine a man in total darkness. He thinks he is in a cellar or dungeon. Then there comes a sound. He thinks it might be a sound from far off—waves or wind-blown trees or cattle half a mile away." And it is then that he realizes that he is not in a dungeon at all, but that he is outside in the open air. Nothing really has changed. He is still in darkness. But now he knows that he is not alone, that he is not a prisoner, that that terrible door is bolted on the inside.

—∭—

That older man who lost his wife to cancer was once a young boy who lost his mother to the same disease. Being only nine and as yet unaware of the depth of God's mercy and grace, the young Lewis did not commit his experience to words. But when the grown man came to write *The Magician's Nephew,* the novel that recounts in loving detail the birth of Narnia, he chose as his hero a young boy named Digory who must watch helplessly as his mother succumbs to an incurable disease. In the novel, Digory enters Narnia through magic and meets its Creator: Aslan the Lion. Seeing the wonder, vitality, and fecundity of this new, innocent, unfallen world, Digory decides that he will ask Aslan if he cannot give him something that will cure his mother and restore her to health.

> Up till then [Digory] had been looking at the Lion's
> great front feet and the huge claws on them; now, in his
> despair, he looked up at its face. What he saw surprised
> him as much as anything in his whole life. For the tawny
> face was bent down near his own and (wonder of
> wonders) great shining tears stood in the Lion's eyes.
> They were such big, bright tears compared with Digory's
> own that for a moment he felt as if the Lion must really
> be sorrier about his Mother than he was himself.
>
> "My son, my son," said Aslan, "I know. Grief is
> great. Only you and I in this land know that yet. Let us
> be good to one another. But I have to think of hundreds
> of years in the life of Narnia." (Chapter 12)

Aslan does not give Digory what he asks, but sends him instead on a mission to retrieve a golden apple that will protect Narnia from the evil that Digory has inadvertently brought into it. At one point Digory is tempted to steal the apple for himself and bring it back to his mother, but he successfully resists the temptation. As he dutifully carries the apple back to Aslan, he suffers a momentary pang of regret over his decision, but when he thinks back on Aslan's tears, he feels assured that he was right not to steal it. With the apple, Aslan plants a tree of protection, and from that tree he gives Digory another apple that he may use to cure his mother.

The young C. S. Lewis was not given an apple from another world to heal his dying mother, for such apples do not grow in this fallen, magic-deprived world of ours. But as he matured into faith and came to know him who is the Aslan of our world, Lewis realized that though Christ does not always deliver us from our tragedies, he always shares fully in our grief. He shed human tears at the tomb of his friend Lazarus, and he sheds the same tears beside the tombs of all those whom he died to save. Indeed, his tears, like those of Aslan, are greater than our own, for he alone was there at the beginning to witness the original plan, the plan that did not require death as the doorway to heaven. He knows both what could have been and what now is, that harder way of sorrow that our rebellion made necessary; in fact, he trod that way of sorrow himself. Christ has experienced—firsthand and in the flesh—what none of the angels, what not even the Father or the Spirit can ever truly know—the full force of evil and of suffering. And because he has, because he has struggled himself with the problem of pain, he can speak to us those words that the sufferer most desperately needs to hear: "My child, I know your grief. Let us be good to one another."

5

Wrestling
with the Arts

The Death of Language

Orthodox Christian faith is grounded in the *Logos* (or Word). Both Christ, who reveals God to us, and the Bible, which reveals Christ to us, bear the title of *Logos Theou* (or Word of God), and we who love and honor Christ and the Scriptures are People of the Word. That is why, of all the challenges faced by the twenty-first-century Christian, perhaps the most dangerous are the modern and postmodern attacks on language. And they are dangerous, for they not only cut at one of the foundations of the faith; they do so in ways so subtle that they fail to register on the radar screens of most believers.

Until the late nineteenth century, nearly all Christians—indeed, nearly all people—simply took for granted that language was inherently meaningful, that behind the words they used was something real. Words like love, justice, and beauty *meant* something; they were names that embodied an absolute or essential meaning, conduits through which streamed a higher, transcendent truth. The user of the words might not be able to grasp the full meaning inherent within them, but the meanings were nevertheless there to be discovered and disseminated. Plato believed that all the things of our earth were but an imitation of a more perfect Form or Idea that existed in the heavens in the eternal, unchanging World of Being. In traditional Western thought, language at its highest pointed back to, and took its ultimate meaning from, these eternal Forms.

Language was one of the main vehicles given by God to mankind to aid in the search for knowledge and understanding. When grouped together into phrases and sentences, words could capture and convey a multitude of meanings and possibilities. Through the medium of lucid, balanced prose, whether thought, spoken, or written, one could build vast structures of logic and reason, explore hypotheses and hunches, and delve into one's own mind, heart, and soul. Through the more ancient medium of poetry, one could range even farther. For poetry, with its figurative language, its precise phrasing, and its ability to load each word with a wealth of connotative meanings, could draw both the writer and the reader up almost to the heavenly realm of Plato's Forms. Through the metaphors and parallelisms and paradoxes of poetry, one could overcome for a moment the curse of Babel and return to the pure, unfallen language of Adam—that mysterious language by which Adam named the animals. Raptured into this higher mode of speech, language ceased to be a mere covering and metamorphosed into flesh.

This traditional faith in the meaningfulness of words and in the ability of language, especially poetic language, to point back to higher truths was not to survive unscathed the revisionist energy of the modern age. Earlier I identified Freud, Darwin, Marx, and Nietzsche as the founders of modernism. To these four we must now add Ferdinand de Saussure (1857–1913), the Swiss linguist who radically altered our view of the function and status of language. In his posthumously published *Course in General Linguistics,* Saussure argues that the relationship between a word and the meaning of that word is not that between a name and some preexistent thing-in-itself that dwelt in Plato's World of Being. Rather, a word (or *sign*) was composed of a physical sound-image (or *signifier*) that pointed back to a shadowy concept (or *signified*). The concept, or signified, has no separate, absolute status apart from the signifier: that is, language is not a naming process by which human beings attach a word to a ready-made idea like truth or beauty that exists apart from and independent of our thoughts about truth and beauty. In this debunking of the existence and even possibility of absolute truth, Saussure is writing in the tradition of Nietzsche, who reduced both the Forms of Plato and the transcendent truths of Christianity to concepts that people (and cultures) "made up" and then forgot they made them up.

Saussure (guided perhaps by Nietzsche's 1873 essay, "Truth and Falsity in an Ultramoral Sense") extended this dethroning of the signified further to assert not only that signifieds have no separate existence apart from the signifiers to which they are attached, but that the relationship between the signifier and signified is arbitrary. There is no essential link between the sound-image "t-r-u-t-h" (signifier) and the concept "truth" (signified); we might just as well have selected a wholly different sound-image to refer to the concept. Of course, the obvious proof that this is so (that the relationship between signifier and signified is always an arbitrary one) is the simple fact that there are so many different languages, each of which uses different signifiers to point to the same signified.

For Saussure there is nothing magical, nothing God-given, nothing essential about the words we use. Language is a man-made structure that works upward from material, physical, natural realities, not a divinely ordained system that descends from above. (Once again, we encounter that modernist paradigm that posits the nature of reality as a bottom-to-top rather than a top-to-bottom phenomenon.) Language does not come into being via some type of revelation; it is not invented by individuals possessed of poetic genius. Indeed, it is not invented at all, if by "invention" we mean the creation of a single, self-conscious mind. Just as modernist textual and classical critics dethroned Moses and Homer as the "creators" of the Pentateuch and the *Iliad,* so Saussure makes it clear that language is a social product over which the individual has no control. It is the linguistic system that makes the poet, not vice versa.

Furthermore, just as the individual cannot invent or use language apart from one's own society, so individual words only gain their meaning in relationship to the linguistic structure that surrounds them. Indeed signs (words) have *no* essential or preexisting meaning apart from the linguistic structure from which they derive their meaning. And that meaning emerges not out of the similarities that link one sign to another, but out of the *differences* that set them apart from other signs within the overarching system. Thus, even such a simple sign as the word "c-a-t" is made meaningful only by the fact that it is not "b-a-t" or "c-u-t" or "c-a-n."

Like most of his fellow modernists, Saussure is also classified as a structuralist—the terms modernism and structuralism are used almost interchangeably by most scholars. As a structuralist, he believed that all meaning, whether philosophical, theological, aesthetic, or linguistic, did not proceed downward from some divine presence but upward from physical structures. And these structures as Saussure and his fellow modernists defined them are social rather than individual, unconscious rather than conscious, material rather than metaphysical, deterministic rather than humanistic. The clearest example can be seen in the structure of language itself. When we speak or write or even think, our words do not come to us via revelation; they are products of an objective, scientific linguistic structure that determines the meanings of our words and thoughts. For Marx and Freud, it is the economic means and modes of production and the deep hidden structures of the unconscious mind that determine the ideology of the state or the ego of the citizen. Nothing exists (or *means*) apart from these structures; indeed, as we saw above, even the individual parts that make up the structure do not possess their own positive meaning but only gain meaning in the fact that they differ from other parts of the structure. To use a modern example: the individual ones and zeros that make up the binary code of a compact disc have no meaning in themselves; yet, when strung together in a system of differences (one is defined as not being a zero, and vice versa), they can "produce" a complex symphony. More radically, our DNA (which forms the genetic structure out of which our personality rises) is composed of a string of "units" (c, a, t, g), each of which, by itself, is meaningless.

But what has all this do with the arts, the purported subject of this chapter? A great deal. The power and function of the arts, especially of poetry, has traditionally rested on their ability to transcend their socio-economic, spatiotemporal structures and grasp at truths that are eternal and unchanging—thus, we say that Shakespeare is not of an age but for all time. Stranded as we are in bodies and in a world that age, decay, and die, the arts are one of the magic doorways that help us glimpse our own immortality. Poetry (which, as it has traditionally been championed as the highest, most divine of the genres, shall be the focus in this chapter) holds out the promise of a pure language untainted by rude, material concerns. Poetry is one of the channels through which we commune with the origins and essences of things, whether those things be physical, emotional, intellectual, or spiritual. In this sense, of course, the Bible emerges as the highest form of poetry, for it claims to bear within its pattern of words, phrases, and images the mind and the will and the plan of God. (Thus, I would hold that in defending the status of poetry, we defend as well the authority of Scripture; but more on this later.)

The structuralism of Saussure would disconnect that divine channel that poetry and the Bible strive to erect. It would teach language its physical limits and its materialist boundaries, would inscribe and circumscribe it within a closed system that offers no escape into the realm of the metaphysical. Still, though structuralism clipped the wings of poetry, it did not effect the total death of language. Though Saussure killed the "illusion" that words can point back to an absolute, eternal meaning, he *did* allow for the possibility of meaning within the confines of the linguistic system. Within the structure, at least, meaning was not wholly arbitrary but was fixed within a fairly stable web of differences. But even this small faith was soon to be shattered by a second wave of revisionary energy that we call, variously, postmodernism and poststructuralism.

—⁊—

At the center of postmodernism lie the writings of French philosopher and critic Jacques Derrida (b. 1930). In his lecture, "Structure,

Sign and Play in the Discourse of the Human Sciences" (1966), Derrida begins with the theories of Saussure but then quickly goes beyond them. Thus, though he accepts Saussure's dual assertion that the relationship between signifier and signified is arbitrary and that words (or signs) are arranged in patterns of difference, he questions Saussure's own "illusion" that within the confines of the linguistic structure meaning is fixed. On the one hand, Derrida applauds modernists like Saussure for breaking away from the traditional belief that an absolute, eternal, originary standard exists which can serve as both the locus and the touchstone against which meaning can be measured. On the other hand, he accuses these same philosophers and linguists of merely replacing this divine standard with material structures that they feel can provide an alternate fixed center for meaning.

The rallying cry of postmodernism is simply this: no center exists. Whenever we try to work our way back to a center, argues Derrida, we find that the center has shifted—that it is, in fact, not a center at all. To put it in linguistic terms, whenever we try to trace a signifier back to a signified, we invariably find that what we thought was a signified is merely another signifier pointing to another signified. Unfortunately, after we trace the second signifier back to the second signified, we find, once again, that what we thought (hoped, prayed) was a signified that could provide us with a *telos* (an end and a purpose) to our quest is, yet again, but another signifier. Meaning, in Derrida's economy, is finally unattainable. Indeed, to attempt to arrive at a fixed origin or center is to lose oneself in an *aporia* (a Greek word that means waylessness) in which meaning is perpetually deferred. As philosopher, linguist, and literary critic, Derrida would break down (or *deconstruct*) the relationship between signifier and signified, and, by so doing, expose the illusory nature of the signified. For the signified *is* an illusion, inasmuch as it purports to ground and freeze the meaning of the signifier. And, just as there are no signifieds, so is there no Transcendental Signified, no final signified-origin-center that can serve as the supreme and primary reference point for all meaning. For the poststructuralist, Nietzsche's cry that "God is dead" carries not only spiritual and philosophical repercussions, but aesthetic and linguistic ones as well.

Earlier I argued that the Pre-Socratic philosophers were in many ways the first proponents of the modernist paradigm. I would argue here that one of the most famous (or infamous) of these Pre-Socratics, Gorgias the Sophist, was the true father of postmodern deconstruction. Gorgias propounded three propositions that embody an ethos and an approach that are startlingly close to those of poststructuralists like Derrida: 1) Nothing exists; 2) If it does exist, it cannot be known; 3) If it can be known, it cannot be communicated. By his first proposition, Gorgias meant not to deny the existence of physical reality but to deny the existence of any absolute, eternal presence that dwells outside of space and time. Proposition two follows with the assertion that even if the gods or the Forms or some other first principle actually did exist, we would be unable to know or perceive those principles. The third proposition completes Gorgias's philosophical skepticism by arguing that even if an individual could somehow come to know one of these first principles, he would be powerless to communicate that knowledge by word, sound, or image to others.

The core theories of deconstruction line up remarkably well with Gorgias's three propositions. In place of "Nothing exists," we have Derrida's claim that there are no Transcendental Signifieds, no divine origins or supernatural presences, no Alphas or Omegas that can act as a center and thus give order and structure to our shadowy world of signifiers. As for the second proposition ("If it exists, it cannot be known"), Derrida's concept of aporia boldly proclaims our inability to find our way back to any fixed meaning or presence. Even if meaning did exist, our knowledge of it would be perpetually deferred. Finally, Gorgias's third proposition ("If it can be known, it cannot be communicated") finds its echo in what Derrida terms the breakdown of signifier and signified. For the purposes of this chapter, it is the third proposition that frames the vital question: can poetry, and the arts in general, capture, or even express, divine meaning and truth?

To the medieval Christian, the answer to this question would have been a hearty and resounding "yea," but the last century has worn the edge off this traditional faith in language. Indeed, if structuralism denies to poetry the ability to embody absolute meaning, poststructuralism denies it the ability to embody any fixed meaning at all. For the post-modernist, language is just too slippery a vehicle for conveying meaning; no clear line can be drawn from signifier to signified. Poetry, like language in general, is just a mess of words—words without form, without structure, without meaning. The words don't take us anywhere; they merely carry us round and round in an endless circle of aporia. The arts thus lose their privileged status as vehicles for attaining a higher vision of truth and become merely another string of signifiers. It was the deconstructionists who first began to refer to all forms of communication, whether verbal or visual, by a single, all-encompassing word: *text.* Their reason for doing so is generally misunderstood by both academic and lay critics who use the word frequently and unconsciously. To refer to everything as text is to deconstruct the traditional hierarchy of genres that would place poetry (especially epic and tragedy) at the top of a pyramid of ascending value, a value based partly on the ability of that genre to embody issues of enduring worth. To include all forms of writing from a Shakespeare sonnet to a television sitcom to a pornographic picture in the same broad category is not to lift up all human communication to the level of Homer, Virgil, and Dante. It is, rather, to pull everything down to an equal level of insignificance. It is to carry out the modern rage for radical egalitarianism to its most ugly, nihilistic, destructive extreme.

—⁂—

The legacy of modernism and postmodernism has not been friendly to poetry, at least in terms of its traditional truth claims, and yet, few Christian voices have been raised in support of the metaphysical status of the arts. Christians—and here I speak specifically of evangelical Protestants who have been outspoken in their criticism of the excesses of modernism and postmodernism—have not fought for poetry with anything like the vigor they have fought for creationism or biblical morality or the authority of Scripture. We are lacking in our defense of poetry, and if we are to wrestle adequately with the postmodern challenge to the integrity of the arts, then we must first try to understand why it is that today's church (particularly the Protestant denominations) has essentially failed in the modern war for words.

The answer to this riddle dates back two centuries. Whether we realize it or not, we are heirs of the Enlightenment, with its privileging of fact over fiction, logic over intuition, external over internal, public over private, history over myth. We (and by we, I specifically mean evangelical Protestants, of which I am one) ascribe far more validity to scientific, rational discourse than we do to the ambiguous, irony-rich language of the arts. Despite the fact that our faith is grounded in a book that is jam-packed with dozens of literary genres, that expresses most of its wisdom in the form of poetry, and that is narrative rather than doctrinal in its essential focus and scope (see the work of such postliberals as Stanley Hauerwas), we yet prefer to embody truth in the form of logical, non-contradictory statements that can be verified along scientific, mathematical lines. We seek in our truth claims a kind of balance, but it is *not* the more aesthetic balance on which Hebrew poetry and most of Jesus' sayings rest (that is, parallelism). Rather, the balance we seek is rational, technical, positivistic.

We seek a language that behaves, one in which there is a strict, one-to-one correspondence between each word and the meaning that the word is meant to convey. As for irony, metaphor, symbolism, paradox, ambiguity—the very life force of poetry—such concepts are to be swept away as so many ancient relics of those unenlightened, medieval, Catholic days of mystery, ritual, and superstition. We claim to believe that the Bible was inspired by God but written by men and that it is, like Jesus himself, fully divine and fully human; yet we act as if the Bible were what the Muslims claim the Koran to be, the exact and literal words of God as they were dictated to a prophet who was most likely illiterate. At times, we can even become iconoclasts, breakers of images who would guard the noncorporeal purity of the invisible God with an Islamic fury. No, we do not actually destroy icons (as did a group of Eastern Orthodox Christians in the eighth century who considered the use of icons in worship a form of idolatry), nor do we smash stained-glass windows (as some of the more radical British Puritans did in the seventeenth century), but we do often insulate ourselves from the images. Like the ancient Hebrews, we hold ourselves separate from all that is slippery.

I intimated above that evangelical thought is in part an outgrowth of Enlightenment ideology, a position that has gained fairly wide acceptance over the last two decades. Among the many fine scholars who have worked in this vein are philosopher Alasdair MacIntyre (*After Virtue*, 1981, 1984), theologian-missiologist Lesslie Newbigin (*Foolishness to the Greeks*, 1986), and historian-sociologist Mark Noll (*The Scandal of the Evangelical Mind*, 1994). In many ways, it is not surprising that evangelical thinkers living in the early twentieth century absorbed an Enlightenment mind-set. Reacting against nineteenth-century liberal theologians and critics who seemed poised to reduce Christianity to a purely emotional, private, even mythic enterprise, American Fundamentalists fought to prove that our faith and our Bible could stand up to the most rigorous tests that science could devise. Unfortunately, in fighting this good fight, they made the mistake of conceding the arena to their opponent. They accepted the Enlightenment split of fact/fiction, reason/emotion, and logic/intuition, and accordingly strove to demonstrate that the Bible belonged firmly on the left side of each divide. Thus, marshalling all the critical tools they had learned from the Enlightenment, they set out to ground the truth claims of the Bible not on a poetic view of inspiration but on a more scientific view of inerrancy, not on narrative explication of God's sacred history but on syllogistic proof texts. The Bible was to be distinguished from poetry and the arts, guarded, in fact, from all those who would interpret it along the lines of literary analysis. Again, they were fighting a good and sincere fight, but they were destined to lose. The Bible simply cannot be held to a system of verification that did not exist when it was written, that has only itself existed for two hundred years.

Is it any wonder that modern evangelicals along with a major portion of orthodox believers seem unable, if not unwilling, to defend poetry from the attacks of modernism and postmodernism? Without realizing it, we have absorbed both a structural and poststructural view of poetry. This is not to say that we have rejected the arts out of hand, but we are too often willing to accept a radically polarized literary world in which there is "secular" fiction purged of all Christian meaning on the one side and overtly and unsubtly "Christian" fiction on the other. Our answer to Saussure and Derrida is too often simply this: Fiction should either not be taken seriously as a vehicle for divine truth or it should shun all slipperiness and merely offer a thinly veiled sermon. Do we desire a fiction where humanism and Christianity, Athens and Jerusalem can meet? Do we yearn for a kind of poetry that, though written from a Christian worldview, does not offer simple, prepackaged meaning? Do we herald the return of complex Christian poets and novelists like Donne, Milton, Coleridge, Browning, Dostoyevsky, Hopkins, and O'Connor who will challenge (rather than simply affirm) our faith? Why can't we rise above our modern aesthetic naysayers to fashion a literature that, while replete with irony, paradox, and ambiguity, can yet assert not in spite of, but *by means of* its "slippery" metaphors and symbols the existence and reality of transcendent truths?

The Aesthetics of Incarnation

Were I to follow the organization of my earlier chapters, I would, at this point, turn over the podium to C. S. Lewis and let him wrestle it out with Saussure and Derrida. Unfortunately, at the time Lewis was writing, the full force of the modern-postmodern assaults on language had not yet made themselves felt in the academic world. Lewis, therefore, never addressed directly the issues raised in the section above. Had he lived today, I feel quite certain that he would have identified deconstruction as a major threat to the status and meaningfulness of poetry (and, by extension, to the status and meaningfulness of the Bible), and he would have mounted an appropriate defense of the arts. But he did not, and so it falls to us as his heirs and "co-wrestlers" to fashion our own defense along the lines laid down by Lewis Agonistes. That is to say, we must cast our eyes backward to the medieval church and seek out a counter-vision of the arts that we can hold up against the "logocidal" fury of the modern and postmodern world.

This is precisely where we must begin, for it is in the older traditions of Western Catholicism and Eastern Orthodoxy that we shall find the raw material for a full and multifaceted defense of poetry and the arts that, far from closing its eyes to the slippery nature of artistic expression, embraces that slipperiness as one of the aspects of the arts that enables them to bear divine or at least supernatural meaning. In this first phase of the argument—what I have been calling the reactive defense—I shall wrestle alongside Lewis rather than through him, a practice that I hope this book will encourage its readers to emulate. Guided by Lewis's penchant for rehabilitating our medieval past and by his intermittent but persistent tendency to push the Incarnation to the center of Christian faith, I shall attempt to construct an aesthetics of incarnation that can provide the twenty-first-century Christian with a theoretical defense against the challenges of deconstruction. Then, in the second phase, the proactive offense, I shall turn fully to Lewis's fiction, where we shall find, perhaps not surprisingly, that Lewis has left us a rich legacy in which this very aesthetics of incarnation has been successfully put into practice.

—∽∾—

In his spiritual autobiography, *Confessions,* St. Augustine documents his slow movement toward Christian faith. One by one, he highlights the various personal and theological stumbling blocks that he had to overcome before he could receive in their fullness Christ, the Bible, and the doctrines of the Church. Among these stumbling blocks is one that is often overlooked by evangelicals. According to the *Confessions* (book 4, chapter 4), Augustine could not accept the authority of Scripture until he learned from St. Ambrose to read the Bible in a spiritual, allegorical sense. Read literally, the Word remained dead and cold to the skeptical, highly learned Augustine; read spiritually, it quickened and came to life (Augustine references 2 Corinthians 3:6). Scriptural passages that had at first seemed unlikely and even absurd became, once the veil of mystery had been lifted from them, sources of revelation to be received with love and obedience by the simple and the learned alike.

This is not to say that Augustine rejected the literal reading or treated the Scriptures as if they were merely a sophisticated myth. He took the Bible at its word when it spoke of historical events and personages, but he sought constantly to pierce through the simple historical sense to reach higher levels of meaning. In his search for these higher meanings, Augustine followed the example of St. Paul who, in his epistles, interpreted the Old Testament in a typological rather than simply historical fashion. According to a typological reading of the Bible, many of the people, events, and symbols of the Old Testament are significant not only in themselves but as types or figures of things to be revealed later. Indeed, these biblical events do not achieve their full meaning until they are viewed in the light of the life, death, and resurrection of Christ and the new covenant (or testament) that God makes with the church. Thus, Joshua (*Yeshua*), who led the children of Israel over the River Jordan and into the Promised Land is a type (or prefiguring) of Jesus (the Greek equivalent of Yeshua) who leads the church through the River of Death into the Promised Land of heaven. Likewise, the near sacrifice of Isaac by his father, Abraham, is a type of the Crucifixion, where God the Father sacrificed his beloved Son. When Jesus reworks and redefines the meaning of Passover at the Last Supper, he engages in a supreme act of typology. Just as the only way for a firstborn son of Abraham to survive the angel of death is to anoint the doorframe of his house with the blood of a spotless lamb, so the only way for a fallen son of Adam to escape divine judgment is to drink the sacri-ficial blood of the sinless Lamb of God. Thus covered by the blood, both the ancient Israelite and the modern Christian are assured that death and judgment will pass over them. Indeed, as St. Paul says, Christ our Passover is sacrificed for us.

To read the Bible typologically is to engage in a type of interpretation that the modernist and postmodernist can partly understand. If we are to treat the first Passover meal as having a multitude of possible interpretations, then we are saying, in effect, that the event is a signifier pointing to a number of different signifieds. From here, however, we quickly part company with the deconstructionist, for, if we have eyes to see, we will realize that the slippery nature of the signifier does not lead us away from meaning into a nihilistic aporia but towards a higher meaning in which the vast patterns of God's divine plan are for a bright, intense moment revealed. Rather than chase each other around in an endless circle, the signifiers line themselves up into a ladder that draws us rung by rung, signified by signified, up a golden chain of ever increasing meaning whose topmost rung is attached to the throne of God.

The power of God's salvation history is too complex, too multi-layered to be contained in a series of one-to-one correspondences in which each signifier attaches itself to one and only one signified. When Isaiah prophesies (7:14) that a *virgin* will give birth to a son and his name will be called Immanuel, it is vital that the Hebrew word he uses can mean both "a literal virgin" and "a young girl." It is vital because Isaiah's prophecy, like most of the prophecies scattered throughout the Old and New Testament, has (at minimum) a double fulfillment. Isaiah's prophecy was fulfilled soon after he made it, when a young girl (perhaps the prophet's wife) conceived and bore a child. But the full import of the prophecy would not be revealed until many centuries later, when a literal virgin named Mary (and the Greek word for virgin can *only* mean "virgin") gave birth to a son who would not bear the physical name Immanuel but would embody the meaning of that name: God with us. It is the slipperiness of the Hebrew word for "virgin" that allows for the dual prophecy and that thus enables the mystery of God's hidden plans to hover over human language as God's glory rested over the outspread wings of the cherubim that adorned the mercy seat of the Ark of the Covenant.

Paul and Augustine both understood that the Bible was not just a textbook but a sacred vehicle for drawing together meaning in rich and complex patterns. Indeed, as the later Church Fathers (particularly St. Thomas Aquinas) studied Pauline and Augustinian typology, they gradually expanded it to encompass even more levels of meaning. During the heyday of the medieval church, nearly every verse of Scripture was believed to work on four separate levels: the literal (or historical), the allegorical (or typological), the tropological (or moral), and the anagogical (or mystical). In the fourteenth century, Dante adapted this fourfold approach to Scripture to serve as one of the groundworks for his *Divine Comedy*. In a famous letter to one of his patrons, Dante explains this theological and aesthetic approach by offering a fourfold reading of the Bible phrase "when Israel out of Egypt came." Taken literally, this phrase refers to the Exodus; allegorically, it signifies how Christ freed us from sin; tropologically, it describes the conversion of the soul from its bondage to sin to its new freedom in Christ; anagogically, it prophesies that final, glorious moment when the human soul will leave behind the body's long slavery to death and corruption and enter the true Promised Land of heaven. As we work our way through these four levels of meaning, our first instinct might be to read them in chronological or ascending order, and indeed, the levels do tend to move us upward from earth to heaven. Still, Dante insists that the levels must finally be read simultaneously, in a single flash of visionary insight. Dante can make this claim, for he believes that the language of Scripture and of poetry at its most sublime is not singular or linear but *polysemous* (Greek for "many signs"). As we saw above, the slippery nature of poetry and of those images, metaphors, and symbols on which all of the arts finally rest is what enables it to hold in tension a supernatural meaning that could not be expressed in a closed, mathematical system where A must always equal B and X can never equal Y.

—⁓—

As the Catholic doctors of the ancient and medieval church were busy demonstrating the polysemous nature of Scripture, the theologians of Eastern Orthodoxy were equally busy endowing the visual arts with a similar weight of earthly and divine meaning. As anyone who has ever studied the history of Orthodoxy or spent time in an Orthodox Church quickly learns, icons are central to the theology and worship of those who look to Constantinople rather than Rome as the spiritual center of their faith. I suppose the simplest definition of an icon would be "a pictorial representation of Christ, Mary, or one of the saints." However, for Eastern Orthodox Christians (whether they be Greek or Russian or Armenian), icons have always meant a great deal more.

The icon is a crux, an axis, a nexus at which physical and spiritual, temporal and eternal meet. At the heart of Orthodoxy as at the heart of any true Christian church lie the twin mysteries of the Incarnation—the belief that Jesus Christ was fully man and fully God, and the

Resurrection—the belief that Jesus Christ rose bodily from the dead. The icon testifies to these sublime truths. As man and God meet, historically, in the person of Christ, so do the human and the divine meet, symbolically, in the physical depiction either of Christ himself or of a fallen man made holy (*saint* in Greek means "holy") through life in Christ. As Jesus effected the redemption and glorification of the flesh through his bodily resurrection (indeed, in Orthodox churches Christ still bears the stigmata he won on the cross), so the icon is a mute but powerful witness to the fact that physical matter can bear and contain divinity and that the natural elements of this world, though subject now to futility, will one day be brought to perfection (Romans 8:18–23).

The icon is a way station, a meeting ground where past, present, and future realities converge. The Christian who stands before an icon and notes the elongated fingers, the strange olive sheen of the skin, and the oddly shaped features like a face seen through flickering candlelight is reminded that at a precise moment in history God entered our world, and by making the invisible God visible, made possible all symbolic art that attempts to capture physically a reality that is spiritual. The Christian who worships in an Orthodox church and feels watched by the eyes of a hundred icons is reminded that in the Mass the divine liturgy is being celebrated in heaven as well as on earth and that when the worshiper sings hymns to God the glorified saints join in praise. The Christian who raises eyes up to the dome to look full upon the massive icon of Christ the All-powerful is reminded that our present reality is temporal, that all things are moving toward a purposeful end, a glorious consummation when death shall be swallowed up by life and when, in the twinkling of an eye, we shall be caught up into the heavens and our weary flesh shall be transformed into the radiant garments of the children of God.

The icon does not, of course, embody divinity in a full and perfect form—only Christ does that. Rather, it is the very fact that God *did* take on flesh in the person of Christ that empowers the arts and enables them to strive toward the divine. As intimated above, Christ, by allying himself with our natural, fallen world of signifiers run amok, baptized physical matter as a fit receptacle for divine meaning and presence. This is why the New Testament, though it continues to forbid idolatry in all forms, does not repeat the specific Mosaic commandment against graven images. If Christ can become flesh without "polluting" his divinity, then it is now permissible for human beings to paint and sculpt images of the Incarnate Christ. For the Muslim, of course, the very thought that God would take on flesh is the greatest of heresies: a fact that explains why the Muslims are the most unapologetic of iconoclasts (they do not allow any kind of representation, even of the prophet Muhammad).

Indeed, any Christian defense of the arts must finally rest on the Incarnation, that most slippery of doctrines. Think of it. In modern linguistic terms, the story of the Incarnation is the story of how the Transcendental Signified became a lowly signifier while continuing to be a signified. In fact, it is the Incarnation and the Incarnation alone that offers the final refutation of Gorgias's three propositions, and, by extension, deconstruction itself. Perhaps the most exalted statement of the Incarnation is to be found in the prologue to John's Gospel (1:1–18), and it is precisely there, in that most beautiful of divine poems, that we find the answer to all three propositions. Thus, in answer to proposition one (nothing exists), we read: "In the beginning was the Word [Logos], and the Word was with God, and the Word was God" (verse 1). In answer to proposition two (if it exists it cannot be known), we read: "And the Word became flesh and dwelt among us, full of grace and truth; we have beheld his glory, glory as of the only Son from the Father" (verse 14). In answer to proposition three (if it can be known, it cannot be communicated), we read: "No one has ever seen God; the only Son, who is in the bosom of the Father, he has made him known" (verse 18).

It is the Incarnation that offers us the firmest faith that absolute truth and divine meaning not only exist but are knowable and capable of being expressed in human language. It is the Incarnation, too, that holds out the promise that we and our language (both verbal and visual) will someday be redeemed from this fallen world of decaying signifiers. Indeed, in contrast to the Synoptics, John's Gospel suggests that the atoning work of Christ was as fully revealed at Calvary as at the stable in Bethlehem. Such a suggestion is a vital one that must be especially grasped by evangelicals who tend to put most of their focus on the

Crucifixion. Christ's death on the cross is, of course, of the utmost importance—apart from it, we are still in our sins—but that death would have been either impossible or ineffectual had the Incarnation not effected the greatest and most wonderful miracle of history—the joining of humanity and divinity in a perfect fusion in which the one does not cancel out the other. The writers of the Apostle's Creed understood the centrality of the Incarnation to our faith, and they devoted most of their theological energies to defining it. The creation of the world, the Atonement, even the Resurrection are each accorded but a single phrase, but the passage devoted to the Incarnation rolls on and on in a symphony of phrases that attempt to define the indefinable, to capture in words that which is almost unthinkable. Nearly all the heresies that plagued the early Church sprang out of a misunderstanding of the Incarnation (now denying Christ's deity, now denying his humanity), heresies that would culminate in the formation of a new religion (Islam) whose rejection of the Incarnation would be total and irrevocable.

Once again, the Incarnation must lie at the core of any attempt to defend and champion the status of the arts. For the arts, in their most exalted form, are nothing more nor less than an attempt to mediate between the spiritual and the physical, the general and the specific, the universal and the concrete. In this sense the sacraments and the liturgical celebrations of Eastern Orthodoxy and Western Catholicism represent the highest form of art, even as they embody and reenact the Incarnation. The Lord's Supper is the most perfect of symbols, the great reservoir of polysemous meaning. The communion wine remains wine, and yet it is also simultaneously the blood of Christ. And yet that blood is itself polysemous, for it is both the physical blood of Jesus of Nazareth that was spilled once for all at Calvary and the eternal blood of the Lamb that has continued to cover sinners for the past two thousand years. The sacraments are like Jacob's Ladder: they build a stairway between earth and heaven upon which the divine presence can ceaselessly ascend and descend. Poetry too, when it is most worthy of itself, is sacramental; it erects its ladders in a thousand different places, striving ever to embody emotions and choices and struggles that can neither be seen nor heard nor tasted in words that are physical, tangible, consumable.

On the one side, then, we have conservative evangelicals who argue that language is meaningful because it is not slippery; on the other we have liberal theorists who claim that it is slippery and therefore meaningless. In the center, I would suggest, we have poetry that cries out on the rooftops that language is more meaningful precisely because it *is* slippery. Indeed, poetry, with its desire to incarnate transcendent truths in material images while yet maintaining via metaphors, symbols, allusions, and other devices a vital sense of play and interchange between the two, comes much closer than science or logic or even systematic theology to capturing and embodying the mystery inherent in the Incarnation.

Now this is not to say that poetry can explain the Incarnation or that it should take the place of doctrines and creeds. It is to suggest, rather, that the aesthetic process by which poetry embodies universal truths in a concrete form is *analogous* to the mystery of the Incarnation. In understanding and experiencing the former, we predispose our hearts and minds to embrace the latter in all its fullness. In a similar way, though sexual intimacy between a husband and wife is not the same thing as the Great Marriage of Christ and the Church that will usher in the new age (Revelation 21–22), the former (as Paul attests in Ephesians 5:31–32) prefigures the latter in that both events involve a mystical union of two into one. As husband and wife become one flesh while yet remaining individuals, so the highest destiny of a Christian is to join in perfect union with Christ while yet retaining his own God-given individuality. Sexuality helps us to understand this great mystery, a mystery which is itself closely allied to the Incarnation.

But the link between poetry and the mysteries of the Christian faith goes somewhat deeper than mere analogy. As was noted earlier, the Bible is jam-packed with poetry, from the Psalms to the Proverbs, from the Song of Solomon to the books of the prophets; even the teachings of Jesus tend to fall into the same parallelisms that define the predominant form of Hebrew poetry. And what of the epistles of St. Paul, whose writings contain the core of New Testament doctrine? If we take up those epistles again and read them with the eye of the artist, we will note that Paul, after building step-by-step a logical edifice of systematic theology, will often veer into the aesthetic and lose himself in a prayer or a poem of intense beauty, as he does, for example, in Romans 8:35–39, Romans 11:33–36, and Ephesians 3:17b–21. Aesthetic-minded Christians like Erasmus were well aware of these moments in Paul and referred to them as O altitudo moments, from the first two words in Latin of Romans 11:33: "Oh, the depth of the riches both of the wisdom and the knowledge of God! How unsearchable His judgments and untraceable His ways!" Though Paul is a master of logical prose, he will quickly wax poetic when faced with the mysteries of love (1 Corinthians 13) or of the Incarnation (Phillippians 2:5–11) or of the Resurrection Body (1 Corinthians 15:35–58).

Poetry and the arts, the icons of Orthodoxy, the sacraments of Catholicism, the books of the Bible: all are but so many types of Jacob's Ladder. And, as such, they point us invariably to Christ who is not only like Jacob's Ladder but is himself Jacob's Ladder in all its fullness. When Jesus promises Nathanael (John 1:51) that he shall see the heavens opened and the angels of God ascending and descending on the Son of Man, he identifies himself both allegorically and literally with Jacob's Ladder (see Genesis 28:12). Jesus Christ (the true Ladder to and Icon of God the Father) is the nexus, the way station, the middle ground where God and man, spiritual and physical, signified and signifier meet and join hands across a divide that was built by sin and that too often is maintained by a strictly rational view of reality. Christ has broken down the dividing wall, and every great poem, sacred or secular, seconds him in his mighty work of spiritual, metaphysical, and linguistic reconciliation.

—⚬—

I have reflected several times on the differences between Christianity and Islam, and have even dared to suggest that when Christians gravitate toward a scientific reading of Scripture or betray a deep suspicion of the arts, that they are embodying an ethos that is more Islamic than Christian. I would like now to explore one final difference that will help us to round out our aesthetics of incarnation, a distinction that runs throughout the Koran and the Bible. Though few Christians realize it, the entire Koran is written in first person from the perspective of Allah; indeed, according to Islam, Muhammad was merely a secretary: nothing of his personality or his culture appears in the Koran. Though the Bible contains many prophetic passages in which God speaks directly, it also includes the varied and unique perspectives of its different writers. Far from a series of divine monologues, the Bible is told mostly from the human point of view. God is always at work, carrying out his plan for humanity, but he generally works in and through human history. At times, as in the book of Daniel, he even works through pagan nations. The dream of the giant which Daniel interprets for Nebuchadnezzar (2:27–45) is like a great mural or an epic poem in miniature that documents how God's purposes are subtly orchestrated through a succession of earthly kingdoms whose leaders neither know nor worship him.

At the heart of the Bible is not a set of doctrines but a story, a sacred narrative of fall and redemption through which run, like the individual threads of a Persian carpet, a thousand different patterns linked together in a vast weave of false steps, recurrences, and typologies. God is the ultimate author of the story, yet it does not run apart from or in opposition to the choices and actions of mankind; on the contrary, it continually calls us to become a part of the story, to find our place in the drama. To each of us God has given gifts and talents, and it is our sacred duty to use those gifts and talents in a manner worthy of the Giver. And, as that Giver is also a Maker, part of that proper use will and must entail artistic creation. That is to say, our role as characters in the divine drama is not only to participate in the vast historical movement from fall to redemption but to embody and recapitulate that movement in works of aesthetic beauty. "[W]e make in our measure and in our derivative mode," writes J. R. R. Tolkien in his long essay "On Fairy-Stories," "because we are made: and not only made, but made in the image and likeness of a Maker." If God is a Creator, then it behooves us—at least those of us with the requisite gifts—to be sub-creators (the phrase is Tolkien's). Perhaps we shall not all create a world as varied and complex as the Middle Earth that Tolkien conjures up for us in *The Lord of the Rings,* but there are many of us who have the capacity to be "world-makers."

As we shall explore in a moment, one of our finest world-makers, a writer who embodied in his life and writings the full glory of the aesthetics of incarnation, is none other than C. S. Lewis.

The Sub-Creator at Work

Though I have spoken now at length about poetry and the arts, I have not yet invoked imagination, that faculty that makes creativity possible. If reason and logic are what allow us to analyze, to make distinctions, to dissect arguments, to build a chain of propositions, then imagination is what enables us to synthesize, to forge connections, to heal divisions, to integrate and humanize knowledge. By reason, we understand our own physical world; by imagination, we create a new one. Through logic, laws are discerned and numbered; through imagination, mysteries are embraced and paradoxes held in suspension. Like faith, imagination helps us to see that which is unseen and embody that which is desired; like love, it helps draw the two into one, for it sees the similarity that lurks in dissimilarity and the reconciliation that is masked by enmity. Imagination at its highest is incarnational; it brings a spiritual vision down to earth even as it lifts up the most mundane of things to the seventh heaven. Without imagination, we could not be the sub-creators that many of us are called to be. For the sub-creator must accomplish five goals: 1) make an analogy between our primary, "real" world and a secondary, aesthetic one; 2) birth that secondary world in an act of loving desire that is unafraid to rest in mysteries; 3) shape that world into a unified whole replete with the kind of purpose and drama that our own Creator imbued our world with at the beginning; 4) afford to the creatures of that world an autonomy and an integrity apart from our own; 5) joy with and suffer with those creatures in an act of sympathetic imagination.

Tolkien does all of these things in *The Lord of the Rings,* and we would not be far amiss if we devoted the latter portion of this chapter to analyzing that great work of the Christian imagination (a work that, like the Chronicles of Narnia, succeeds splendidly in that rare hybrid genre of popular/serious, religious/secular fiction that includes Dante's *Divine Comedy,* Chaucer's *Canterbury Tales,* and Spenser's *Faerie Queene,* and that our age could use a good deal more of). However, Lewis is finally our best candidate, for he, in his fiction, not only perfected the role of sub-creator but understood and enacted that role in terms of that aesthetics of incarnation that I laid out above.

I previously explained that Lewis's road to Christianity did not begin in earnest until he read George MacDonald's *Phantastes* and felt his imagination baptized. It was Lewis's acceptance of Christ and the Bible that enabled him to reengage his sense of wonder and to reclaim his earlier love of myth. The mature Lewis in his many roles as teacher, scholar, apologist, and novelist would never again allow his reason and his imagination to stand in enmity with one another; rather, he would allow the former to be deepened and humanized by the latter and the latter to be informed and authorized by the former. Lewis would place the Incarnation at the very center of his faith not just because of its theological necessity but because he saw it as the grand miracle in which every thread of the divine tapestry and every scene of the sacred drama came together (see especially chapter 14 of *Miracles*). The Incarnation promised unity both in the inner world of Lewis's once divided psyche and in that outer world of spiritual and aesthetic wonder that did not fully open itself to Lewis until he embraced the Incarnate One as his Savior. Indeed, it was in great part his meditations upon the Incarnate Christ that empowered Lewis to see reality on two levels: the spiritual and the earthly, the sacred and the profane. He brought his vision not only to his readings of such Christian poets as Dante, Spenser, and Milton, but to his own fiction as well.

In his three monumental attempts at an incarnational fiction (the Chronicles of Narnia, the space trilogy, and *Till We Have Faces*), Lewis constantly shifts between two realities that traffic back and forth as dramatically and dynamically as the angels descending and ascending on Jacob's Ladder. In the first, Narnia and our own world are held up as icons of each other; in tracing Narnia's sacred history, we gain insight into our own narrative, without effacing the reality and integrity of the former. In the space trilogy, physical and spiritual struggles are seen to parallel and interact with one another, and the events that occur on Earth, Mars, and Venus are so drawn together that they function as various levels of the same archetypal pattern. In *Till We Have Faces,* perhaps Lewis's most mature work, we enter fully into a pagan, pre-Christian tale in which every element of the story points in some way to Christ and to grace, not because Lewis builds a one-to-one correspondence between the characters and events of his novel and those of the Bible, but because when we look back on the pagan tale from our post-Resurrection perspective, we *see* the latter *in* the former, just as we see the Lord's Supper in the Jewish Passover. In all three cases, meaning is slippery and polysemous, as it is for the deconstructionist, but it is nevertheless grounded in a Transcendental Signified who is the ultimate author of all the dramas. Each novel builds its own closed referential system in which each event (or signifier) is bound to every other in a pattern of sameness and difference. However, whereas the structuralist would build this system from the ground up, the larger significance that gravitates around such events as Aslan's sacrifice, the temptation of the Queen of Perelandra, or the marriage of Psyche to the beast radiates from above.

Although Lewis died two decades before deconstruction seized hold of the academy, he knew well the importance of celebrating and preserving the arts as a vehicle for keeping open that dialogue between higher and lower that mumbled in the myths of the Greeks and spoke clearly at Mount Sinai, that was established firmly and for all time in the Incarnation, and that yet persists in the sacramental life of the church. He sought successfully to make such a vehicle of his own fiction (oddly, he was never able fully to achieve this goal in his first love, poetry), and our age, if it is to wrestle effectively with the challenges of poststructuralism, would do well to study and imitate his example.

When Aristotle wrote his *Poetics* in the fourth century B.C., he hoped that by identifying the characteristics that made fifth-century B.C. tragedy so great, he might inspire a new Golden Age of drama. In imitation of Aristotle, I shall close this chapter by exploring four elements of the Chronicles of Narnia which render these seven novels a veritable blueprint for that incarnational aesthetic our age so desperately needs.

—∞—

First, the Chronicles, as Lewis often insisted, are *not,* technically speaking, allegories. In chapter 2 of his first academic work, *The Allegory of Love,* Lewis makes a distinction between allegory and symbol that can help us understand the exact meaning of this rather odd insistence. In a pure allegory like *Pilgrim's Progress* or Lewis's own *Pilgrim's Regress,* Lewis explains, the characters and incidents function simply as pictures whose sole purpose is to illustrate an internal passion, temptation, or similar struggle or characteristic. When a character in a medieval drama is caught in a dilemma and must choose between the hard way of virtue and the simple way of vice, the storyteller will often allegorize the invisible struggle in the form of a visible angel on the character's right shoulder and an equally visible devil on the left. In this example, the angel and devil are not real characters with unique backgrounds, beliefs, and destinies; they are merely material embodiments of an immaterial struggle between good and evil. In symbolism, however, this movement from immaterial struggle to material embodiment is reversed. The struggle is now something concrete—a person or an event or an object—that is used to point upward to a reality that is unseen, that lies just outside our grasp. The purest example of symbolism, which Lewis also calls sacramentalism, is the Lord's Supper, where physical bread and wine are made to bear all the mystery and awe of the body and blood of Christ. For Lewis, symbolism is yet another Jacob's Ladder mediating between the physical and the spiritual, the earthly and the heavenly. It works on two levels simultaneously without allowing the one to cancel out the other.

The human and animal heroes of the Chronicles cannot be reduced to mere Christian allegories, for they possess their own separate life and integrity apart from the events and characters of the Bible. Yes, Aslan is partly an allegory of Christ, but he is also a very real lion who has his own history, his own reality, his own metaphysical status. Aslan is Christ while continuing to be Aslan, just as the communion wine becomes the blood of Christ while never ceasing to remain wine. Even so was the Virgin Mary a very average rustic girl who also happened to bear in her womb all the fullness of God's presence.

The people and events that move their way through the seven Chronicles of Narnia are polysemous: as signifiers, they point in several different directions at once. Narnia itself is a metaphor for our own primary world while yet retaining the full integrity of a secondary, self-sufficient world fashioned by a human sub-creator who would second his own Creator in the magic art of world-making. When Aslan is killed on the Stone Table, we are, of course, meant to link his death to the Crucifixion of Christ, but when we read the account, it is nevertheless Aslan we weep for. As Lewis explains in many of the letters that he wrote to his child fans, rather than make Aslan a simple allegory for Christ, he asked himself what form Christ might take if he were to incarnate himself on another world. Aslan is not Jesus of Nazareth but the Christ of Narnia; just so, in the second novel of the space trilogy (*Perelandra*), Ransom, while remaining a normal, fallen man, becomes the Christ of Venus. How, *The Lion, the Witch and the Wardrobe* asks, would the sacred drama play itself out on a world of talking animals that is held in the icy grip of a tyrannical White Witch? Why not, if I may use the terms of this chapter, take the Christian belief that the Transcendental Signified became a signifier and reenact that descent in a world whose system of signifiers parallels (rather than simply copies) our own?

Prince Caspian is, in part, a novel about what happens when a system of signifiers is allowed to decay and become corrupted—to become "slippery" in the negative sense of the deconstructionists. A thousand years have passed since the death and resurrection of Aslan and the kingship of the four earth children, and the new rulers of Narnia, the human Telmarines, have either relegated these events to nonhistorical myths or (more insidiously) linked the old signifiers of wood and water, which were good forces in *The Lion, the Witch and the Wardrobe,* to a new set of signifieds that are evil and foreboding. Like the post-Enlightenment, post-Christian Europe in which Lewis lived and wrote, Narnia has forgotten her heritage and has unwoven the subtle tapestry of her most sacred signifiers. By reentering Narnia, the four children help restore balance and meaning to these signifiers, even as Lewis the author, by creating a world that parallels the salvation history of the Bible, helps those of us living in a postmodern age to reassemble and reweave our own patterns of sacred signifiers.

And this leads us to the second element of the Chronicles that renders them an ideal embodiment of the aesthetics of incarnation. Though the seven novels *do* parallel many of the deepest truths of Christianity, Lewis did not set out to write a book that would do so. Indeed, as he explains in "Sometimes Fairy Stories May Say Best What's to Be Said" (anthologized in *On Stories*), Lewis did not set out to write a Christian work at all. The Narnia books began for Lewis with a series of recurring images ("a faun carrying an umbrella, a queen on a sledge, a magnificent lion") that haunted his dreams and pressed on him to embody them in some written form. Once Lewis accepted the task of incarnating these images, he next searched for the appropriate genre to give them form. He decided early on that the images could not rest properly in a genre that demanded a love interest, psychological analysis, or philosophical digressions. In the end, he was drawn to the fairy tale as "the ideal Form for the stuff [he] had to say."

Then, Lewis explains, having chosen his genre and having begun to arrange the images into a narrative, the Christian within him began to wonder if these images could not be used as a vehicle for "smuggling" Christian principles into a post-Christian age. That is to say, once Lewis the artist was satisfied with his genre, Lewis the man began to shape that genre in accordance with his own deepest passions and beliefs:

I thought I saw how stories of this kind could steal
past a certain inhibition which had paralysed much of
my own religion in childhood. Why did one find it so
hard to feel as one was told one ought to feel about God
or about the sufferings of Christ? I thought the chief
reason was that one was told one ought to. An obligation
to feel can freeze feelings. And reverence itself did harm.
The whole subject was associated with lowered voices;
almost as if it were something medical. But supposing
that by casting all these things into an imaginary world,
stripping them of their stained-glass and Sunday school
associations, one could make them for the first time

appear in their real potency? Could one not thus steal
past those watchful dragons? I thought one could.

One of the things that Lewis and Tolkien discovered as they discussed their mutual love for fairy stories and their mutual disappointment that no one seemed interested in writing them anymore, was the shocking conclusion that they themselves would have to write the very stories they most desired to read. In fashioning his Chronicles, Lewis not only accomplished this goal but succeeded in fulfilling a related one, which was to present the Christian message in a way that he wished it could have been presented to him when he was a child. In an act of redemptive deconstruction, Lewis disassociated the signifieds of Christian theology from their typical, uninspiring signifiers (their Sunday school associations) and attached them instead to a new set of signifiers with the power to reinvigorate and inspire young and old alike.

By so doing, he managed to avoid the false dichotomy between secular and Christian fiction that has marginalized—if not ghettoized—many Christian artists and severely restricted their palettes. The Chronicles of Narnia are not one or the other; they are both simultaneously. Because the Chronicles, like most of the Bible, are narrative rather than propositional, because they embody their message more in the actions and interactions of characters than in heavy-handed sermons, they can be read and enjoyed *as* secular stories by those who know nothing of their spiritual dimensions. Yet, the extra dimension remains in the form of a spiritual potential energy ever ready to be released. The unbeliever who works through one of Bach's sacred pieces may experience only its formal beauty and power; nevertheless, in experiencing that, the listener has also received without even realizing it the higher levels of meaning latent in the work. These latent meanings will lie dormant, and though for many this sleep will be an eternal one, for others the sleeper will someday arise, sprout wings, and soar up the aesthetic ladder to glimpse the Transcendental Signified. Such is the experience of many, myself included, who read the Chronicles as a child solely for their stories, and then read them again as an adult to be stunned into wonder by their deeper Christian message, a message made all the more real because it had already been experienced in childhood in a purely aesthetic way.

Indeed, Lewis often advised parents *not* to enumerate all the Christian parallels for their child. Better to let the child learn to love Aslan in a fresh, simple, unmediated way, and then later in the fullness of time, as it were, transfer that love to Christ. To spell out all the parallels from the beginning would be to risk erecting the same Sunday school associations that Lewis had so diligently tried to break down. When Lucy is told in the final chapter of *The Voyage of the Dawn Treader* that she will not be returning to Narnia, she is greatly saddened, not so much because she will never see Narnia again as because she fears she will now never see Aslan again. In reply, Aslan tells her that she must return to her own world, where she will learn to know him by another name. That name, of course, is Jesus, a name Lucy will come to love even more because her experiences with Aslan have taught her, in part, how to love one who is both all mighty and all loving.

I said a moment ago that Lewis succeeded in breaking down these associations by fashioning a whole new set of signifiers to embody the teachings of Christ, the Bible, and the church. As part of this process of re-signification, Lewis incorporated into his Chronicles stories and figures from a number of different Christian and pagan traditions: Jewish history, Greco-Roman mythology, Norse sagas, Arthurian legends, and medieval romances. This thrilling if somewhat eclectic aspect of the Chronicles (which marks the third of the four elements under consideration) was sadly rejected by Tolkien (that most pure and single-minded of sub-creators), who thought the Chronicles hastily written and a bit of a grab bag. To do Tolkien justice, it is true that Lewis never really attempted to synthesize these diverse traditions in a systematic way. But then this is something that Lewis never intended to do.

The links that Lewis sought to forge between the various traditions that converge in his Narnian novels went far deeper than mere surface consistency. Lewis's desire was not to build his seven-part epic on a scientific, Enlightenment type of inerrancy that would not allow for any logical contradictions. Rather, he sought a richer, more poetic, more *human* type of synthesis in which all the various elements would find their consistency, not on the level of a mathematical, one-to-one correspondence, but on the spiritual and aesthetic level of mythic archetypes.

We have already explored Lewis's key belief that all of the greatest mythic heroes, from Balder to Osiris to Adonis to Mithras, embody man's innate need for a divine/human Savior and thus find their historical fulfillment, rather than their contradiction, in the person of Jesus Christ. In keeping with this belief, Lewis allows the yearnings of each tradition as they are embodied in the waking dreams of each nation and people group to dialogue with each other in a redemptive way. For most readers this dialogue will only register on an unconscious level as a feeling of the rightness and "fittedness" of the various yearnings that underlie the different traditions.

For those, however, who have eyes to see and ears to hear, a greater revelation will unveil itself. Though each spiritual-cultural-mythic tradition works within its own seemingly closed system of signifiers and signifieds, they are all finally a part of that greater "signification system" that finds its Transcendental Signified in the triune God who is also the Incarnate God—the two-in-one out of the three-in-one, as Dante, the greatest archetypal Christian poet, would put it. Indeed, Dante offers us a supreme example of such converging signification systems in *Inferno*, Canto II, when he has Virgil reveal that while the pagan Aeneas thought he was laying by the power and guidance of Jupiter, the foundation of Rome, he was in fact being used by the Christian God to begin a historical process that would result in the Roman Catholic Church. Just so, Nebuchadnezzar's dream of the giant reveals to us that whereas the rulers of the four kingdoms of Babylon, Persia, Greece, and Rome thought that their respective deities were "calling the shots," both kings and gods were but minor musicians in that vast concert of history whose orchestrator and conductor is God and God alone.

In the Chronicles, all the different characters and episodes are eventually linked to the person and will of Aslan. He is the one behind all the stories, the one who gives them all their meaning and purpose. He is the hub out of which all the spokes proceed and return. Just as Colossians 1:17 tells us that in Christ all things consist, so is Aslan the glue that holds together Narnia, the one around whom all the signifiers group themselves. Aslan is the inspirer and the fulfiller of dreams, the one who calls and the one who guides, the one who warns and the one who saves.

Aslan interacts with Narnia and its visitors on every level of meaning, often providing the true signifieds to signifiers that the characters have misinterpreted. And once we as readers grasp and *feel* how wide is the ministry of Aslan, we will be better able to return to our own world and experience again that God in whom we live and move and have our being. We may even be empowered to see, perhaps for the first time, that Christ is the true Alpha and Omega, not only of our theological and philosophical beliefs, but of our individual and cultural dreams.

And this leads us, in turn, to the fourth and final element of the Chronicles that make them the ideal model for twenty-first-century Christian artists seeking to embody in their work an aesthetics of incarnation. Aslan is truly a type in the Pauline and Augustinian sense of Christ, but not only for the obvious reason that he does and says many of the things that Christ said and did. Aslan is a type of Christ because he inspires in us the same kind of numinous awe that Christ does. When we read of how Aslan was sacrificed on the Stone Table, we receive more than a theological primer of the Crucifixion; we viscerally experience the pain and sorrow of Calvary. When the Stone Table cracks and Susan and Lucy turn to see Aslan risen from the dead, his shorn mane restored to its golden purity, we feel many of the same emotions that the women who went to the tomb must have felt on Easter morning when the angels told them the glorious news that he whose body they came to anoint was not there but risen.

In one of the most memorable scenes from *The Lion, the Witch and the Wardrobe* (chapter 7), Lewis tells us that when the four children first hear from Mr. Beaver that "Aslan is on the move," it works a mysterious spell upon them:

> None of the children knew who Aslan was any more
> than you do; but the moment the Beaver had spoken
> these words everyone felt quite different. Perhaps it has
> sometimes happened to you in a dream that someone
> says something which you don't understand but in the
> dream it feels as if it had some enormous meaning—
> either a terrifying one which turns the whole dream into
> a nightmare or else a lovely meaning too lovely to put

into words, which makes the dream so beautiful that you
remember it all your life and are always wishing you
could get into that dream again. It was like that now. At
the name of Aslan each one of the children felt
something jump in his inside. Edmund [the traitor of
the group] felt a sensation of mysterious horror. Peter
felt suddenly brave and adventurous. Susan felt as if
some delicious smell or some delightful strain of music
had just floated by her. And Lucy got the feeling you
have when you wake up in the morning and realise that
it is the beginning of the holidays or the beginning of
summer.

Reading this passage, one can almost imagine that it must have been the inspiration for that wonderful gospel song that begins: "Jesus, Jesus, Jesus; / There's just something about that name." Just the name of Aslan draws out of the children their most intimate yearnings and desires, their deepest hopes and fears. A new element has entered into their mental, emotional, and spiritual landscape, one that seizes control of that landscape and reorients everything in it around itself. Something which a moment before was wholly unknown to the children is immediately apprehended as that thing which they have always longed for, wished for, waited for. That thing may be overwhelmingly beautiful or terrifyingly dreadful, but its coming has not gone unannounced, at least in that deepest part of ourselves out of which myths and dreams and visions arise. And when it comes, it brings with it an atmosphere of sacredness that cannot be denied—though it can be resisted.

One aspect about Aslan that Lewis comments on several times in the Chronicles is that when the children are in his presence, they feel happy and serious, joyful and solemn at the same time. Many today, even those who worship in sacramental churches, have lost this sense that Christ is both a friend whom we can laugh with and the king of the universe before whom every knee on earth and heaven and under the earth shall someday bow. We have lost our sense of awe, a loss that is felt as much in the realm of the arts as in the theology and worship of the Christian church. It is no great surprise that language has been slowly ceding its integrity and meaningfulness. How can we find meaning in the signifiers when we no longer know how to respond to the signifieds, much less the Transcendental Signified? Lewis carries us to the threshold of that renewed response we so desperately need when he helps us to understand that Aslan is not a tame lion; though he is loving and good, he is certainly not safe. Aslan, like Christ himself, may be embraced, but he is by no means to be trifled with.

The author of Hebrews has a similar lesson to teach us about that sacred Word which is both the Incarnate Son and the linguistic record that bears him witness: "For the word of God is living and effective and sharper than any two-edged sword, penetrating as far as to divide soul, spirit, joints, and marrow; it is a judge of the ideas and thoughts of the heart. No creature is hidden from Him, but all things are naked and exposed to the eyes of Him to whom we must give account" (Heb. 4:12–13). Words have power, and if we are to revive and restore the arts to their proper place as lesser versions of Jacob's Ladder and the Incarnation, then it is time we learned again to feel reverence for the Logos in all its manifestations.

Wrestling with Heaven and Hell

The Deconstruction of Heaven and Hell

Of all the core teachings of the Christian faith, the one that perhaps causes the most discomfort among post-Enlightenment Americans and Europeans is the doctrine of hell. The modern mind, non-Christian *or* Christian, simply cannot fathom how a loving God could condemn someone to eternal punishment, nor how any place like hell could actually exist. Hell, with its attendant demons, strikes the modern as an ancient relic of barbaric superstition, a nasty little fairy tale used to scare naughty children who refuse to do their chores or mind their parents. Satan is merely a character from the stage, not the embodiment of evil and rebellion; and the temptations that he whispers in our ears are merely products of our own subconscious lusts and egos. And in any case, if Satan *were* a real being, he'd more likely be the tragic hero than the wretched villain. We are, after all, rather fond of rebels, especially if they stand up, underdog-like, against an authority that seems to our mind to be harsh or illegitimate. Thus, though Satan is meant to be the "bad guy" of *Paradise Lost,* many critics since the early nineteenth century starting with the British Romantic poets William Blake and Percy Bysshe Shelley have hailed Satan as the true hero of Milton's epic and have even suggested that Milton himself was of the devil's party without knowing it.

Hell is distinctly not to our liking, and many churches and denominations have tried to brush it quietly under the rug. However, while Christians (hoping, in part, to attract the nonbeliever) have downplayed the doctrine of hell, the secular world has simultaneously deconstructed the traditional Christian faith in heaven. Though it might seem that all people, whether they accept the Christian revelation or not, would naturally gravitate toward the idea and promise of heaven, the Western secular establishment has essentially dismissed it as a primitive form of wish fulfillment. Heaven is at best pie-in-the-sky, at worst, a political and theocratic delusion used to keep the masses in their place.

There have always, of course, been people who doubted the existence of heaven and hell, just as believers and nonbelievers alike have struggled with evil and suffering since time began. But the intensity of the doubt, just like the fervor of the struggle, has increased manyfold over the last two hundred years and has threatened to eat away at two of the main pillars of the Christian faith. This threat has made necessary a fuller and more nuanced attempt to defend heaven and hell from skeptics, naysayers, and those "more sensitive" people in the congregation whom the church has expended far too much energy attempting to pacify and accommodate. In mounting an apology for heaven and hell that the modern can understand, there is no better ally and fellow wrestler than C. S. Lewis. Both in his apologetical works and his fiction (and particularly in those two works that fall in between: *The Screwtape Letters* and *The Great Divorce*), Lewis explores not only the nature of heaven and hell itself but of the choices that lead us to those opposing destinations.

Before turning to Lewis Agonistes, however, we must first pause to consider why it is that the modern and postmodern world, in contrast to earlier ages, has felt such a strong need to dilute, alter, or reject the orthodox biblical notions of heaven and hell. Only once we have understood the full nature of the opponent can we enter the arena with any hope of winning the agon.

—∞—

Though the Enlightenment was born out of a French culture that was strongly hierarchical and aristocratic, it paved the way for a modern ethos that privileges equality as one of the highest of all values. We are all the same, and we should all be treated the same—so runs the liberal, egalitarian mantra. Of course, all we who live in free societies that honor and protect individual rights owe a great debt of gratitude to this legacy of the Enlightenment, as long as we don't forget that the Enlightenment, for all its questioning of orthodox Christianity, would not have been possible apart from a belief in the inherent worth and dignity of every human being, a belief whose ultimate sources are Christ and the Bible. Still, modern notions of equality have gone so far that they have forced even believing Christians to question the doctrine of hell.

"It's not fair that some should go to heaven and others to hell," we cry, believing firmly that our anger has been riled up because our sense of justice has been violated. And yet, more often than not, what really has been outraged is not our sense of justice but our sense of equality. We cannot accept that some will experience eternal bliss while others will be confined to eternal misery. Such a thought smacks of favoritism, of privilege, of unequal treatment; it places one group on the inside and the other on the outside. No wonder moderns are uncomfortable with the idea of a postmortem division into hell and heaven. How can those who balk at temporal distinctions—whether they be hereditary titles, old boy networks, or income inequities—accept anything so drastic as an eternal distinction? We much prefer universal salvation, a concept that fits in more smoothly with that universal brotherhood of man and fatherhood of God that has been the default religion of Europe (and less so of America) for the last two centuries.

With the shift from modernism to postmodernism, this obsession with equality has become even more pronounced. Most moderns, at least, accepted the existence of fairly fixed standards of morality and thus of the possibility and identifiability of sinful and immoral behavior. But the postmodern has pushed the equality envelope to include even moral standards and behavior. What is immoral for one person may be moral for another; what one calls a sin another may call a virtue. No one has the right to judge what is sinful and what is not, for there exists no removed, fixed, "objective" point of view from which to judge, no Tao, to use Lewis's term. At first this inability to judge right from wrong may sound like a reiteration of Jesus' command not to judge, but it is not. The postmodern does not forbid judgment because he recognizes that we are all fellow sinners who must stand before a holy God, but because he finally rejects any real belief *in* a holy God against whom all can be measured and before whom we all must answer for our sinful choices and actions. In fact, with the help of modern science, our postmodern age is poised to do away with moral accountability altogether. Every year, a new report comes out that attempts to link sinful (or at least illegal) behavior to some inescapable genetic defect; immorality is not the result of sinful choices but of the biological determinism of a selfish gene or a violent gene or an infidelity gene. (Of course, it should be added that despite their claims, postmodern relativists *do* judge; they merely direct their righteous anger at sins against equality rather than sins against morality; thus all forms of inequity, from fascism and apartheid to racism and sexism to tax cuts for the wealthy, are branded as immoral.)

Our age is a strange one. We insist vociferously that all individuals have the right to choose whatever they think is best for them, yet we simultaneously absolve ourselves of accountability for those actions. We desire individuality without distinctions, choices without consequences, rewards without opposing penalties, academic recognition without the possibility of failure. We would eat our cake and have it too. We would take full credit for our good actions, while simultaneously absolving ourselves of any bad actions by either blaming those actions on genetic or societal forces outside our control or by merely redefining the bad action so that it ceases to be bad. Like the college student who feels he deserves the "A" simply because he has paid for the class and has "done his work," the modern feels that all people deserve heaven simply because they have lived and have suffered somewhat in their lives.

So goes one school of postmodern thought, but there is another school which is more closely allied to the New Age and to more ancient forms of gnosticism. The former school deconstructs hell by rejecting fixed moral standards and thus eliminating moral accountability; the latter does it in a more subtle, "mystical" way by accepting hell and then reducing it merely to a state of mind. William Blake, he who claimed that Milton was of the devil's party without knowing it, has given us the fullest expression of this second school of thought in his radically imaginative work, *The Marriage of Heaven and Hell*. According to this highly cryptic work, hell is not an intrinsically terrible place. It only appears terrible to us because we allow our perceptions of it to be colored by a religious, pharisaical worldview that exalts reason, order, and obedience and demonizes energy, creativity, and excess. If we could only free ourselves from this worldview and embrace that energy which the religious so fear, we would see that hell is a place of peace and beauty. Indeed, heaven and hell are to be defined neither as places of reward or punishment, nor as the presence or absence of God, but as the products of a certain way of perceiving reality. For Blake, things are not as they are but as they are perceived; it is we, through the mediation of our senses and perceptions, who create the world around us and not vice versa. To quote the central line of the *Marriage*: "If the doors of perception were cleansed every thing would appear to man as it is, infinite. For man has closed himself up, till he sees all things thro' narrow chinks of his cavern." This, of course, sounds a lot like the oft-repeated biblical injunction that we must have eyes to see and ears to hear, and, in fact, it does bear some resemblance to it. For Blake, however, seeing is finally an end in itself; it defines its own reality rather than bringing itself in line with God's fixed standards and his eternal statements on what reality *is*.

Hell as it is depicted in the Bible is, for Blake, an idea, an illusion, a creation of a certain mind-set that would stifle that creative, revolutionary energy that empowers the poet, the lover, the rebel, and the genius. Anticipating by a century Nietzsche's argument that religion is a slave ethic used by the weak to keep the powerful in check, Blake asserts in his *Marriage* that those "who restrain desire, do so because theirs is weak enough to be restrained; and the restrainer or reason usurps its place and governs the unwilling." Hell is but a mental construct imposed upon us by weak-willed people who fear our charisma, our will to power. They convince us that energy is bad and that it will lead us to hell, and we internalize their vision and allow it to color all of our perceptions.

Blake's *Marriage* was written in the final decade of the eighteenth century. As the nineteenth century moved toward its own close, Sigmund Freud was busy taking Blake's notion of heaven and hell as opposing states of mind and undergirding it with his own radical notions of the nature and function of the subconscious. Blake's dichotomy between energy and reason is absorbed deep into the recesses of the unconscious mind to emerge as the *id* (the instinctual life force) and the superego (the moral conscience that would hold the id in check). Unlike the *ego* (which must balance the call of energy and reason, instinct and conscience, and choose the course of action), the id and superego are cut off from reality. The superego in particular is not the voice of God or the embodiment of absolute, eternal moral codes, but the internalization of religious restrictions and social mores. Our belief in and images of heaven and hell are but illusions conjured up by the superego: hell as a threat to hold back the advances of the id and heaven as a reward to those who behave in a socially acceptable way. Heaven has no real, metaphysical existence; it is just the product of subconscious wish fulfillment. Indeed, even hell can be defined as a type of wish fulfillment for superego-led people who enjoy the thought that those who break from society's rules will get their "just deserts."

Though a majority of Americans and at least a large minority of Europeans still hold to a belief in heaven, however variously defined, "serious" academic thinkers and empirical, "common sense" scientists tend to dismiss it as an illusion, and may even look down on the Christian for his "mercenary" belief in a heavenly afterlife. In these tendencies, they have been helped by the nineteenth century faith in science, technology, and progress. An age intent on building utopia (heaven on earth) is sure to have little patience with any talk of pie-in-the-sky-by-and-by and to consider those who look past earth to heaven as traitors to the cause. It is on earth that we shall find Paradise, or not at all—so goes the idealistic vision that has driven many a reformer since the

Enlightenment. And when that day arrives, when mankind builds its universal, utopic state and eliminates all war, poverty, and ignorance, then shall immorality cease, and all shall dwell together as equals. It sounds like a heavenly vision, but it is actually quite the opposite. It is, in fact, a *substitute* for the Christian notion of heaven that does away with the need for hell and that places man (rather than God) on the central throne as author, finisher, and standard bearer. We've come a long way, baby.

The Psychology of Sin

C. S. Lewis understood well the modern discomfort with hell. In chapter 8 of *The Problem of Pain* he admits that most moderns find it a "detestable doctrine," but he never compromised on the absolute necessity of hell within the theological framework of Christianity. Yes, hell might at first seem unfair and might even seem to run counter to a biblically founded belief in the equal dignity of all human beings, but in truth it rests on one of the central mainstays of human dignity, our ability to choose. Again and again, and in book after book, Lewis asserts that hell is *always* something that we choose. If there is a division, it is a division that we knowingly embrace; if there are distinctions, they are distinctions that we ourselves have chosen to adopt. The poverty of the twelve disciples, of St. Francis, and of Mother Teresa does not represent a violation of equal treatment for all; they chose their poverty as a vital part of their calling and embraced it willingly. In an equal and opposite way, those in hell also chose to be where they are; they are those who choose darkness over light, their own will over that of God.

Though Lewis fully embraced salvation by grace through faith, he firmly rejected the belief that God's grace is irresistible. For Lewis, God is the greatest of gamblers. He took a great risk when he chose to give us free will, and he is a good enough gambler to let the chips fall where they may. "I willingly believe," writes Lewis in *The Problem of Pain* (chapter 8), "that the damned are, in one sense, successful, rebels to the end; that the doors of hell are locked on the *inside*. . . . They enjoy forever the horrible freedom they have demanded." Heaven is not some upscale health spa open only to those with six-figure incomes and corporate connections; heaven is for anyone, rich or poor, who wants to be continually in the presence of God. For those who do not desire to dwell in the pure light of God (a light which both warms and exposes), who prefer rather to spend eternity with themselves and their sins, heaven is not really an option. Once we make the choice to reject God and his grace and to embrace forever our own self-centeredness, we leave ourselves with very few options. Indeed, there is really only one place we can go, one place alone where God is not, and that place is called hell. In a way, God loved us so much that he permitted one spot in the universe where he is absent, so that all those who do not desire to spend eternity with him may have a place to go. "In some sense," writes Lewis in his finest sermon, "The Weight of Glory," "as dark to the intellect as it is unendurable to the feelings, we can be both banished from the presence of Him who is present everywhere and erased from the knowledge of Him who knows all. We can be left utterly and absolutely *outside*—repelled, exiled, estranged, finally and unspeakably ignored."

But of course it need not be like this. Just as Lewis asserts emphatically that hell is always something we choose, so too does he repeat over and over in his works that if we truly desire and yearn for heaven, we will not miss it. A lovely promise this, and yet it raises a related question. How is it possible that someone could actually yearn for hell rather than heaven? Or to put it another way, how can someone willingly choose a sinful course of life that will lead to hell, and just as willingly refuse to accept the grace that is its remedy? There have been theologians in the past who have attempted to answer this question, but a philosophical or theological explanation is not really the kind of answer that our age most needs. What we need to hear and understand is how it is *psychologically* possible that someone could choose a sinful course of life that leads to hell. And it is precisely here that C. S. Lewis is the most helpful, for he, perhaps alone among Christian writers, has truly explored the psychology of sin.

According to Lewis, what ultimately drags us down to hell is not a single grand sin that puts us beyond salvation, but a succession of little sins that pulls us bit by bit away from God and his grace. Sin is not so much a single, irredeemable action as it is a slow and insidious *process.* Apart from the Chronicles of Narnia, Lewis's best loved book may well be *The Screwtape Letters,* that remarkable collection of epistles sent by a senior devil, Screwtape, to his nephew, Wormwood, with the purpose of instructing him in the fine art of temptation. As a young, eager tempter, Wormwood hopes to snare his human prey in a major sin, but his uncle advises him to stick to "small" sins instead:

> You will say that these are very small sins; and
> doubtless, like all young tempters, you are anxious to be
> able to report spectacular wickedness. But do remember,
> the only thing that matters is the extent to which you
> separate the man from the Enemy [God]. It does not
> matter how small the sins are, provided that their
> cumulative effect is to edge the man away from the Light
> and out into the Nothing. Murder is no better than cards
> if cards can do the trick. Indeed, the safest road to Hell is
> the gradual one—the gentle slope, soft underfoot,
> without sudden turnings, without milestones, without
> signposts.

Most picture hell as a pit into which we are thrown for one unforgivable sin; Lewis would encourage us to see it rather as a marsh or swamp into which we slide, one peccadillo at a time. The road to hell is a gradual one; indeed, it is the very gradualness of the process of sin that makes it so dangerous. Bit by bit, little by little, we draw ourselves away from God, never realizing that in the process we are slowly dehumanizing ourselves.

Now when I follow Lewis's lead in using the word *dehumanize,* I don't mean it in some limited sociopolitical or psychological sense. A life lived apart from God's grace that seeks only itself to please and that prefers its own egocentric desires over the mercy of Christ is one that will cause us, in the end, to cease to be human. Lewis reminds us in *The Problem of Pain* that, according to the parable of the sheep and the goats (Matthew 25:31–46), the eternal fires of hell were prepared not for sinful human beings but for fallen angels (verse 41). If we are truly human, we will attain heaven. But that, of course, is the point. The people in hell are no longer human beings; they are insubstantial ghosts who have given away their humanity through a self-centered life devoted to the pursuit of sin and the worship of the self:

> To enter heaven is to become more human than you
> ever succeeded in being on earth; to enter hell, is to be
> banished from humanity. What is cast (or casts itself)
> into hell is not a man; it is "remains." . . . hell was not
> made for men. It is in no sense *parallel* to heaven: it is
> "the darkness outside," the outer rim where being fades
> away into nonentity. (*The Problem of Pain*)

In *The Great Divorce* (chapter 3), Lewis compares the souls of the damned to "man-shaped stains." They are like dirty smears on a windowpane—one can "attend to them or ignore them at will." The modern concern over the nonegalitarian nature of hell is here exposed for the delusion that it is. Hell does not embody a violation of the equal dignity and value of all humanity; on the contrary, it is the sinners themselves who have violated their own dignity and humanity by willingly giving it away.

—∞—

But how, we still ask. How *exactly* does one dehumanize oneself? To answer this question we must turn fully to the book mentioned above, *The Great Divorce*. In this imaginative mini-epic, Lewis takes us on a fanciful bus ride from hell to heaven, allowing us to eavesdrop as the souls of the blessed attempt to convince the souls of the damned to forsake their sin and pride and enter heaven. Given the scenario that Lewis sets up, one would expect that all the sinners would rush to accept the offer to leave hell and remain in heaven. As it turns out, only one out of a dozen or so souls accepts the offer; though the damned souls now see the truth and beauty of heaven stretched out before them, they nevertheless choose to return to hell. We are tempted to ask, where is the psychology here? How can a person possessed of full knowledge of heaven and hell yet choose hell? Lewis does not shy away from this question, but answers it through a finely modulated series of "case studies." As we listen with Lewis to each of the dialogues, we are given direct insight into the desires and choices of each of the damned souls. We learn who they are and what motivates them and are able to discern why it is that they are finally powerless to break from their sin and embrace the mercy offered to them.

In the simplest yet perhaps most profound of these case studies (chapter 9), Lewis ponders the damned soul of a garrulous, grumbling old woman who won't cease her "pity-party" long enough to listen to the saint sent to help her. On and on she drones, her petty complaints so numerous and so endless that the poor blessed soul can barely get a word in edgewise. To Lewis, she does not seem an evil woman—only a grumbler. But this, Lewis is told, is the whole point: The question to be asked is whether she is a "grumbler or only a grumble." If there's even an ember of humanity left inside of her, the angels can nurse the flame till it blazes again, but if all that is left is ashes, nothing can be done. The problem is not that the woman is beyond salvation, for God's grace is quite powerful, but that there is nothing left in her to save. She is no longer a human being; she is only the remains of what used to be a woman made in the image of God.

Those who reject hell often do so because they link hell in their minds with a false image of God as a bat-wielding bogey in the sky just waiting for us to slip up so that he can cast us, screaming, into the fiery pits of hell. The case studies that run throughout *The Great Divorce* suggest a different image of God. According to this image, when God looks down on us from heaven, he does not see primarily our sin, but that spark of humanity, that divine breath that lies deep within us, shrouded and suffocated by layers of sin. He desires to blow on that spark and allow it to burn bright and clear, but we, in our rebelliousness, reject his aid and instead snuff out the spark ourselves. In the case of the grumbling woman, she extinguishes her spark through a simple process of entropy. With each grumble, with each outbreak of renewed unthankfulness to the God who created her and died to save her, she sacrifices another piece of her humanity. Bit by bit, she flits it away, like a boy who slowly whittles at a stick until there is not one shred of wood left. We have all seen the process, if not in ourselves then in the lives of our relatives and friends. A man begins by developing a grudge against another person; others beg him to let the grudge go, but he nurses it instead, making it a central part of his being, his identity, his reason for living. In the end, he *becomes* his grudge, just as an angry man becomes his anger or a vain woman becomes her vanity. What was human slowly drains away, and all that is left is the grudge going on forever and ever. The process is so sad, so terribly unnatural that we want to pity the sinner and fight for his rights and his dignity. But how can we? When the final curtain falls, and the sinner finds that he is no longer a sinner but merely his sin, then that human being whom we would pity and defend will have ceased to exist. One can hardly pity a grudge or a grumble.

But flitting away our humanity is not the only method by which sinners dehumanize themselves. In some of his other case studies, Lewis shows us that an equally effective method for snuffing out our divine spark is to forsake our first love (see Revelation 2:4). This spiritual and psychological truth is best illustrated by an incisive dialogue in which a redeemed painter, now a Spirit, tries to convince a former earthly associate and fellow painter, now a Ghost, to join him in Paradise. When he catches his first glimpse of the landscape of heaven, the Ghost immediately yearns to transfer it to canvas and kicks himself for not having remembered to bring his paints. In response, the Saint begins to laugh and exclaims, "'That sort of thing's no good here.'" He then goes on to explain:

> "When you painted on earth—at least in your earlier days—it was because you caught glimpses of Heaven in the earthly landscape. The success of your painting was that it enabled others to see the glimpses too. But here you are having the thing itself. It is from here that the messages came. There is no good *telling* us about this country, for we see it already. In fact we see it better than you do. . . . [Later on] there'll be some things which you'll see better than anyone else. One of the things you'll want to do will be to tell us about them. But not yet. At present your business is to see. Come and see. He is endless. Come and feed."

But the visitor from below is still not satisfied. He insists on knowing *when* he can start painting. The conversation then continues:

"Why, if you are interested in the country only for the sake of painting it, you'll never learn to see the country."

"But that's just how a real artist *is* interested in the country."

"No. You're forgetting," said the Spirit. "That was not how you began. Light itself was your first love: you loved paint only as a means of telling about light."

"Oh, that's ages ago," said the Ghost. "One grows out of that. Of course, you haven't seen my later works. One becomes more and more interested in paint for its own sake."

"One does, indeed. I also have had to recover from that. It was all a snare. Ink and catgut and paint were necessary down there, but they are also dangerous stimulants. Every poet and musician and artist, but for Grace, is drawn away from the love of the thing he tells, to love of the telling till, down in Deep Hell, they cannot be interested in God at all but only in what they say about Him." (Chapter 9)

The Spirit, of course, is right. We are all first drawn to the arts by a desire to grab hold of something that we perceive as being just out of our reach, that ineffable light that beacons to us from just behind the furthest hill. It's the light, the truth, the mystery, the yearning—the joy, Lewis would say—that we desire, not the artistic media in and of itself.

But the Ghost has forsaken his first love, has converted the arts from a royal road to the light to an end in itself; we might almost say a dead end in itself. The Ghost has lost any initial desire he once had to seek the source of the light, which is God. Even if the Ghost were allowed to remain in heaven, he would be unable either to enjoy or receive it. To him, heaven and God are merely subjects to be studied, not realities to be embraced. The Spirit offends and pains him with his silly talk of light and reality. In the end, the Ghost runs back to hell because he has heard that a new artistic "ism" has replaced the older one in which he worked, and he is eager to write another paper or mount another exhibit that will revive his faded reputation. Again, the case study leaves us with a feeling of great sadness. The painter stands in the midst of the very country from which his first love, the love of light, originates, but he has lost the ability to see it. He is alone with himself and his art; the human being who once yearned and desired, who was made to merge with the light and spend eternity in the presence of God, has, like the grumbler, ceased to exist.

Some, then, flit away their humanity, while others simply forsake it. There is a third group, as well, whose ranks are far greater, whose dehumanization is the direct result of a sin which the Bible condemns more often than any other—idolatry. Though we moderns and postmoderns no longer bow before idols of wood and clay, we yet indulge in this oldest of sins every time we take something human and make it in to our God. Instead of desiring God and heaven as they are and for themselves, we seize hold of an earthly thing and shape it into a substitute God, a surrogate heaven. The prevalence and danger of idolatry has always been a common theme among preachers and theologians; what Lewis adds to this theme is the seemingly counterintuitive argument that when the idol is a good thing (patriotism, mother love, charitable activity) rather than a bad thing (drugs, alcoholism, promiscuity), it is often more likely to pull us away from God. The man who is caught in the grip of substance addiction or the woman who is trapped in a cycle of abusive sexual relationships knows full well that their lives were made for more than this. Like the tax collectors and prostitutes of the Gospels, when they encounter Jesus, they are eager to trade their broken lives and shattered dreams for the grace God offers them. But the moral, upright, respected members of the community who have devoted their lives to defending their country or nurturing their children or serving the needy can easily convince themselves that this is the best life has to offer. Like the Pharisees, when Christ appears, they are likely to reject him, for they feel that they are already doing God's will and need no further assistance from Christ. "Brass," writes Lewis, "is mistaken for gold more easily than clay is." Good things make better counterfeits than bad things. Indeed, the greater the virtue, the greater the vice it can become when it is divorced from God and set up as its own idol. Satan, we must remember, was not a thief who made it big, but a fallen angel whose previous glory has made his corruption all the more ugly and deadly.

To illustrate the spiritual and psychological truth of this, Lewis allows us in *The Great Divorce* to contemplate an all-too-familiar case study of a damned soul who has made an idol out of one of the noblest of emotions. The soul is that of a typical middle-class doting mother who has taken the bus to heaven to see her son. Upon arrival, she insists on seeing him immediately, but is told that she must learn to desire God first before she can have her son back. She grows indignant, insists that "God is Love" and that any God that would not let her see her son, must be a false one:

> I don't believe in a God who keeps mother and son
> apart. I believe in a God of Love. No one has a right to
> come between me and my son. Not even God. Tell Him
> that to His face. I want my boy, and I mean to have him.
> He is mine, do you understand? Mine, mine, mine, for
> ever and ever. (Chapter 11)

To her mind, there is nothing more holy than her mother-love; indeed, she has made that very love *into* her God. Her son, or, more exactly, her smothering, manipulative love for her son is the only God that she acknowledges and serves. If God gets in the way of that, he must go; if God won't step aside, then, horrible as it may sound, she's ready to drag her son down with her to hell where she can really care for him.

In a similar case study (chapter 10), Lewis takes us into the mind of a wife who has, like the mother, devoted all her energy and identity to molding her husband into a respectable and successful man. Her ceaseless molding only succeeded in making her husband miserable, but she does not care. She considers him her cross to bear and has made a religion out of her wifely sacrifice. In the end, she, like the mother, is ready to carry him back with her to hell where she can finish the process that she began on earth.

One of the central warnings that runs throughout Lewis's *The Four Loves*, as well as *The Great Divorce,* is that any earthly love, when it is raised up and worshiped as divine in itself, quickly transforms itself into an idol. "Love," he writes at the close of chapter 3, "having become a god, becomes a demon." Yes, God is love, but if we switch that statement around and make love into our God, we will eventually lose not only God but ourselves in the process. We will cease to be human and be cast, along with all the other human "remains," into that lake of fire which was never made to house humanity.

—∞—

What, we must now pause to ask, do all these case studies have in common? All of them, in one way or another, present us with figures who are thoroughly narcissistic. Though love has been defined in many ways, perhaps the best way to define it is as the movement out of narcissism. God, who is the only being in the universe who has the right to be narcissistic, demonstrated love when he moved out of himself to create the world. Two thousand years ago, in an even greater act of love, God again moved out of himself, but this time more radically, more dangerously. He left behind the safety of the Trinity and incarnated himself as a human being. If we are to understand and embrace the love of God, then we, too, must learn to move out of ourselves. Unfortunately, this is exactly what the narcissist cannot do. The narcissist's world, love, and desires are all defined by self-centered egocentrism, an inability to move beyond narcissistic needs and desires. Narcissists cannot even begin to step outside themselves, and if they cannot do that, if they cannot let go of themselves and their sin, then they can never open wide their arms to receive the love and grace of Christ. In the end, writes Lewis in chapter 9 of *The Great Divorce,* there are really only two kinds of people: "those who say to God, 'Thy will be done,' and those to whom God says . . . '*Thy* will be done.'" There is no middle ground. Either we surrender our hearts and minds to God and by so doing become more ourselves, or we choose ourselves over God and eventually lose our humanity.

But beware, warns Lewis, heaven and hell work backwards. Once you have made the choice between yourself and God and have, as a result, been either cast out from or invited into his eternal presence, it will be as if you had always been in hell or heaven:

> That is what mortals misunderstand. They say of some temporal suffering, 'No future bliss can make up for it,' not knowing that Heaven, once attained, will work backwards and turn even that agony into a glory. And of some sinful pleasure they say, "Let me have *this* and I'll take the consequences": little dreaming how damnation will spread back and back into their past and contaminate the pleasure of the sin. Both processes begin even before death. The good man's past begins to change so that his forgiven sins and remembered sorrows take on the quality of Heaven: the bad man's past already conforms to his badness and is filled only with dreariness. (*The Great Divorce,* chapter 9)

In the end, Lewis concludes, the damned will say they have always been in hell, and the blessed shall say they have always dwelt in heaven. The separation is an eternal one, but it is based on a distinction that we ourselves create each time we choose to move toward or away from the grace of God. Heaven and hell are not so much wish fulfillments as they are reality fulfillments. Thus far I have spoken as if each sin or surrender we choose to make draws us closer to hell or heaven; what really happens, in fact, is that each choice we make transforms us bit by bit either into a hellish or a heavenly creature. The struggle between id and superego does not sublimate itself into illusionary visions of eternal punishment or eternal bliss; rather, the struggle molds us into certain kinds of people who are either unable or able to move out of ourselves toward God.

Americans have the wrong understanding of heaven and hell. We think that life is like college and that if we get an "A" we go to heaven, and if we get an "F" we go to hell. Thus, to go to hell is to be a failure, a "loser," and no American can stand to be labeled as such. But the fact of the matter is there are *two* colleges: the College of Heaven and the College of Hell. If we enroll in the former, it means that what we truly desire is God and the things of God. And if that is our desire, Lewis asserts, we shall someday find it: "No soul that seriously and constantly desires joy will ever miss it" (chapter 9). But if we enroll instead in the latter college, it is because we have chosen our own wills over that of God, because we have agreed to adopt as our motto that most American of phrases, "looking out for number one." I have met many people who say they cannot believe in God because he sends people to hell. Invariably, though, as we speak further, it is soon revealed that this person does not like God and certainly does not wish to spend eternity with him. We can't have it both ways. Our souls are immortal; they must go *somewhere* after we die: if not to God, then, by default, they must go to hell. For, as we already said above, hell is the only place in the universe where God is not. And yet, even in hell, God extends some mercy. Hell, as Lewis tells us in book 10, chapter 4 of *The Pilgrim's Regress,* is in part a tourniquet that God wraps around sinners lest they continue to bleed and wound themselves even more.

And without that tourniquet, they *would* wound themselves far more, for in hell they will bleed eternally. There have been a growing number of orthodox and even evangelical believers, John Stott among them, who have argued that hell is not eternal and that the souls of the damned will eventually be annihilated. I do not think that Lewis, were he alive today, would embrace this school of thought, though he would certainly respect the motivation behind it. True, the souls in hell will lose their humanity, but that does not mean they will also lose their immortality. The life God breathed into us at Creation is an indestructible one—indeed, this breath is what sustains all living things—and his promise to clothe us in resurrection bodies is a universal one, whether or not we choose to spend eternity in his presence. If, as the Bible seems to suggest, God has not annihilated any of the purely spiritual angels, then how can we imagine that he will annihilate immortal spirits fused with eternal bodies? And then, of course, there are the characteristics of eternity itself. Eternity does not mean time running perpetually onward; it means being outside of time, living in a suspended present. In the eternal moment of heaven, all is joy and life and praise; in the eternal moment of hell, all is emptiness and sterility and narcissism. There is neither beginning nor ending in heaven and hell; there is no such thing as "semi-eternity." If the damned exist at all in the eternal state of hell, then they must exist there eternally (this is partly why Lewis can claim that heaven and hell work backwards). Conditional immortality is not a divine paradox, like the Incarnation, but a nonsensical contradiction. Lewis reminds us in chapter 2 of *The Problem of Pain* that "meaningless combinations of words do not suddenly acquire meaning simply because we prefix to them the two other words 'God can.'" Still, even if we grant that both heaven and hell (and those who inhabit them) live eternally, we must remember that the *quality* of those two states of eternity is vastly different.

Hell, though it exists and is eternal, is an insubstantial place, a place of ignorance and stagnation. Lewis compares it, in the opening chapters of *The Great Divorce,* to a dingy, drizzly, gloomy little town frozen in a perpetual twilight. It is almost completely devoid of people, for the residents of hell are so quarrelsome and self-centered that they cannot bear to live more than a few days in close proximity to a neighbor. Instead, they continue to move farther and farther out, placing more and more distance not only between themselves and other people, but between themselves and the bus stop that offers them passage to heaven. Napoleon, that supremely egocentric leader, has moved so far from the bus stop that it would take a journey of fifteen thousand years to reach him! In hell, there is neither community nor family nor friendship. There is only eternal narcissism. And yet, Lewis tells us, if you were to ask these people about themselves and their destiny, they would answer, not that they are residents of hell, but that they have always served their country or sacrificed for their career or, above all, been true to themselves.

When Lewis (the character in the fantasy, not the author) hears this, he wonders for a moment if what William Blake wrote in his *Marriage*—that heaven and hell are only states of mind—might not be true. But he is admonished by his heavenly guide, who turns out to be none other than George MacDonald, he who first baptized Lewis's imagination and thus opened his eyes to greater spiritual realities that the damned are blind to. MacDonald (who is also the speaker of many of the excerpts quoted above) resolves Lewis's dilemma in a passage that is central to the entire work:

> Hell is a state of mind—ye never said a truer word.
> And every state of mind, left to itself, every shutting up
> of the creature within the dungeon of its own mind—is,
> in the end, Hell. But Heaven is not a state of mind.
> Heaven is reality itself. All that is fully real is Heavenly.
> For all that can be shaken will be shaken and only the
> unshakable remains. (Chapter 9)

Yes, heaven and hell are states of mind, but they are two very different states. The vision which sees and enters heaven is outwardly directed and yearns upward for reality and truth; the vision which sees death and enters hell is inwardly directed and egocentric. It is profoundly narcissistic and cannot see beyond itself and its own petty concerns.

The title of Lewis's book has often provoked puzzlement among his fans. What is so great about divorce, they are tempted to ask, and what has it to do with heaven and hell? Lewis titled his book *The Great Divorce* because he meant it to be, in part, an answer to Blake's *Marriage of Heaven and Hell.* Lewis would have us understand that heaven and hell are not only real but that they can never be reconciled. They are complete opposites, and no esoteric vision or secret wisdom can bring them into harmony. We postmoderns much prefer both/ands to either/ors, but heaven and hell, Lewis asserts, lie firmly in the latter category. Blake tries to convince us in his work, that if the doors of perception were cleansed, we would see everything as infinite; Lewis counters that Blake's vision is not one that opens doors but closes them, "shutting up the creature within the dungeon of its own mind." Visionary insight is not an absolute good; rather, as with the Colleges of Heaven and Hell, there are two different kinds of vision. The vision which saves is drawn away from itself toward God, toward heaven, toward the light; the vision which damns turns inward to hide and sulk in the darkness.

Like the Pharisees in John 9, the damned are even more blind precisely because they claim that they see. In one of his many pre-Nietzschean moments, Blake once exclaimed: "I must create a system or be enslaved by another man's." The words have a noble ring, but they embody an attitude toward God, toward the world, and toward people, indeed, toward anything outside the self, that if pursued to the end will lead to hell. In the final analysis, MacDonald explains to Lewis:

> A damned soul is nearly nothing: it is shrunk, shut
> up in itself. Good beats upon the damned incessantly as
> sound waves beat on the ears of the deaf, but they
> cannot receive it. Their fists are clenched, their teeth are
> clenched, their eyes fast shut. First they will not, in the
> end they cannot, open their hands for gifts, or their
> mouths for food, or their eyes to see. (Chapter 13)

This is what we make of ourselves when we choose sin and the self over God. This is the upshot of narcissism. This is the psychology of sin.

But I find now that I have grown weary of hell. The time has arrived to leave behind that shriveled, insubstantial realm of ghostly remains and ascend toward the reality that is heaven. In Screwtape's final letter, we discover that the man Wormwood was assigned to tempt has died in a bombing raid in World War II London and ascended to heaven. With horror and disgust in his voice, Screwtape describes what the man must have felt at the moment of his ascension:

> . . . as if a scab had fallen from an old sore, as if he were
> emerging from a hideous, shell-like tetter, as if he
> shuffled off for good and all a defiled, wet, clinging
> garment. By Hell, it is misery enough to see them in
> their mortal days taking off dirtied and uncomfortable
> clothes and splashing in hot water and giving little
> grunts of pleasure—stretching their eased limbs! What,
> then, of this final stripping, this complete cleansing?

Heaven, as MacDonald explains to Lewis, is the very opposite of a state of mind; it is that which is real, that which cannot be shaken. It is what remains when all that is false and dark and impure has been stripped away. To this place, I shall now, on wings borrowed from C. S. Lewis, attempt to ascend.

Our Desires Are Too Weak for Heaven

"We are very shy nowadays," admits Lewis, "of even mentioning heaven."

> We are afraid of the jeer about "pie in the sky," and
> of being told that we are trying to "escape" from the duty
> of making a happy world here and now into dreams of a
> happy world elsewhere. But either there is "pie in the
> sky" or there is not. If there is not, then Christianity is
> false, for this doctrine is woven into its whole fabric. If
> there is, then this truth, like any other, must be faced,
> whether it is useful at political meetings or not. (*The
> Problem of Pain,* chapter 10)

Heaven is, indeed, woven into the fabric of Christianity. Far from a spiritual carrot on a stick that is dangled before the believer to keep him on track, it represents the end, goal, and consummation not only of the Christian walk but of our very creation. We were not made to live in a fallen world, and no matter how well we deploy our technology and how perfectly we build our shining cities of glass, we will nevertheless remain strangers and sojourners on this earth. Indeed, if there is anything that matches the description of the Freudian wish fulfillment, it is precisely our human desire to build a utopia, a heaven on earth. The dark desires of our subconscious finally point us in the direction of self-sufficiency, of a human conquest over all obstacles. The real wish fulfillment that sublimates itself out of *both* our id and superego is an earthly immortality apart from any accountability to God.

But there is something deeper than our subconscious, something within us that yearns for a supernatural glory, a divine beauty, a spiritual light that our world cannot supply. It is that yearning that tells us most of what we know about heaven, and yet, that yearning must not be interpreted (as Freud interpreted the subconscious) as the origin of heaven. Quite to the contrary, our yearnings are but echoes of that greater heavenly reality we have never seen. They are, writes Lewis in "The Weight of Glory," "the scent of a flower we have not found, the echo of a tune we have not heard, news from a country we have never yet visited." *The Problem of Pain* describes their essence:

> . . . that something which [we] were born desiring, and
> which, beneath the flux of other desires and in all the
> momentary silences between the louder passions, night

> and day, year by year, from childhood to old age, [we]
> are looking for, watching for, listening for. . . . [that]
> unattainable ecstasy [that] has hovered just beyond the
> grasp of [our] consciousness.

We experience that yearning throughout our lives; it comes to us in glimpses that Lewis calls joy. The young Lewis's experiences of joy were what supplied him with his first intimations of heaven and set him on his long path to the person and grace of Christ. Lewis later built his greatest and most original apologetic, the argument by desire, upon these moments of joy. Here now we see that joy is the theme, the leit-motiv that runs throughout the life and work of C. S. Lewis.

Like Reepicheep, the chivalrous mouse of *The Voyage of the Dawn Treader* who has joined the crew that he may sail to the utter East and find Aslan's country, which to a Narnian is tantamount to heaven, Lewis spent all of his postconversion (and much of his preconversion) life groping forward in search of that magical country from which joy springs as light and as swift as a bird in flight. He yearned for that greater, heavenly beauty, not just that he might see it, but that he might pass in to it and join with it. Indeed, he boldly proclaims in "The Weight of Glory," that this is the hidden desire that we *all* harbor deep within us, to be one with that joy and beauty that lie shimmering just outside our reach: "That is why we have peopled air and earth and water with gods and goddesses and nymphs and elves—that, though we cannot, yet these projections can enjoy in themselves that beauty, grace, and power of which Nature is the image." Lewis is referring to the myths and legends of the ancient pagan world, but he is also identifying—whether con-sciously or not—what truly drove him to write his own fiction, particu-larly the Chronicles of Narnia. Heaven is what lies behind every fairy tale; it is what we all long for when we are most ourselves.

Many accuse Christianity of holding out heaven as a bribe and Christians of being nothing more than mercenaries. Certainly many preachers have preached on heaven in this manner, but if they have, they have misunderstood their own doctrine. They have failed to realize that heaven is our true home, and that a person can hardly be considered a mercenary for wanting to return home. A mother may bribe her child with a piece of candy, but she does not bribe him, nor does she make a mercenary out of him when she tells him that once he stops pouting in the backyard, he can come back in the house. His home is where he belongs, and while he remains outside sulking in the garden, he is somehow less than himself. The younger son in the parable of the prodigal son (Luke 15) only ceases to be a mercenary when he comes to his senses and heads back home. In "The Weight of Glory" Lewis explains it this way:

> Money is not the natural reward of the lover; that is why
> we call a man mercenary if he marries a woman for the
> sake of her money. But marriage is the proper reward for
> a real lover, and he is not mercenary for desiring it. A
> general who fights well in order to get a peerage is
> mercenary; a general who fights for victory is not,
> victory being the proper reward of battle as marriage is
> the proper reward of love.

We must be ever vigilant lest we fall into the Freudian trap of confusing the cause with the effect, the source with the echo: our yearnings are not the origin of heaven; rather, it is heaven that inspires our experiences of joy. To desire heaven is merely to seek that which first sparked the desire. Like the lover and the general, true believers can seek heaven without shame, for heaven is the proper reward and end to their search. Marriage, victory, heaven: all are fitting consummations of the desire that preceded them.

Our answer, then, to the Freudians and their fellows who deny heaven must be centered around desire, but here we run into a problem. Far too many Christians believe that the very thing that will prevent us from achieving heaven *is* our desires. Many, in the name of a puritan, ascetic holiness, will mortify their desires and stifle their joy, hoping that when the last shred of passion has been ripped out of them, they will be taken up into heaven. But that is the way of Buddha, not of Christ. Heaven is not a stoic, Nirvana-like state that lies beyond pleasure and pain; it is a realm of pure love, joy, and rapture. Heaven is not the absence of desire but the perfection of it. No, if we miss heaven, it is not because our desires are too strong, but because they are too weak for the immense, soul-shattering joy of heaven. "We are half-hearted creatures," writes Lewis in "The Weight of Glory," "fooling about with drink and sex and ambition when infinite joy is offered us, like an ignorant child who wants to go on making mud pies in a slum because he cannot imagine what is meant by the offer of a holiday at the sea. We are far too easily pleased."

The trouble with all those nineteenth-century visions of utopia is not that they are too wonderful for us poor sinners, but that they are too dull for creatures made in the image of that transcendent God who fashioned the universe. Mark Twain was not far wrong when he accused Christians of picturing themselves doing in heaven the very things they hated doing on earth. How often we try to reduce heaven into something less than the earth, when we should be celebrating it as something infinitely more. I fancy that when Christ said that in heaven we shall neither marry nor be given in marriage (Matthew 22:30), it was because heaven is a place where our capacity for love will be so enlarged that we will be able to love all our fellow heaven dwellers with greater ardor and *agape* love than we could the single spouse to whom we were wedded on earth. The Bible tells us to discipline our bodies, not so that we may cast them off when we get to heaven as things alien to the soul, but that we may be better prepared to wear and *enjoy* those glorious resurrection bodies that God has in store for us. Lewis writes in chapter 16 of *Miracles* that the "small and perishable bodies we now have were given to us as ponies are given to schoolboys. We must learn to manage: not that we may some-day be free of horses altogether but that someday we may ride bare-back, confident and rejoicing, those greater mounts, those winged, shining and world-shaking horses which perhaps even now expect us with impatience, pawing and snorting in the King's stables."

Heaven promises to give us to the utmost what Jesus promises his followers in John 10:10—life to the full. But the promise is even more splendid than that: not only life in its fullness and abundance, but life unsullied by even the smallest blot of darkness, misery, death, or decay. Indeed, hell is a tourniquet, but it is also a quarantine. In chapter 13 of *The Great Divorce,* Lewis asks MacDonald the question that has troubled many a modern and postmodern believer: How can those in heaven be truly happy as long as one person is suffering and miserable in hell? The concern behind the question is admirable, filled with all that liberal, egalitarian sentiment that our age so cherishes, but MacDonald quickly rebukes Lewis for his folly. Would he allow the miserable to hold the blessed forever in check? Shall we give to those who refuse to be happy the power to spoil forever the joy of heaven?

> I know it has a grand sound to say ye'll accept no
> salvation which leaves even one creature in the dark
> outside. But watch that sophistry or ye'll make a Dog in
> a Manger the tyrant of the universe. . . . Every disease
> that submits to a cure shall be cured: but we will not call
> blue yellow to please those who insist on still having
> jaundice, nor make a midden of the world's garden for
> the sake of those who cannot abide the smell of roses.

Have we not all had the experience of going on an outing with our extended family and having our joy sullied by a single spoiled child? The naughty child decides that she is not going to enjoy herself, and then proceeds to make sure that none of the others enjoy themselves, either. How splendid to think that in heaven such badly behaved children will be strictly off limits! Yes, if they choose to remain in their misery for all eternity, that terrible choice will be granted them. But they will be forbidden to spread that misery to those in heaven. Heaven means pure freedom. Once there we shall escape not only the tyranny of sin and death, time and space, but the often greater tyranny of those cynics, skeptics, and prudes who, in the midst of love, joy, and life, can only cling desperately to their bloated egos, their anxious fears, and their endless spite.

—✂—

In chapter 14 of *The Voyage of the Dawn Treader,* Reepicheep the Mouse declares for all to hear what he is willing to risk in order that he may find his heart's desire, to come at last to the shore of Aslan's country:

My own plans are made. While I can, I sail east in the *Dawn Treader*. When she fails me, I paddle east in my coracle. When she sinks, I shall swim east with my four paws. And when I can swim no longer, if I have not reached Aslan's country, or shot over the edge of the world in some vast cataract, I shall sink with my nose to the sunrise and Reepicheep will be head of the talking mice in Narnia.

Verily I say unto you, except your desire shall exceed that of Reepicheep, ye shall in no wise enter the Kingdom of Heaven.

Conclusion

Seeing Past the Lines

In his sermon "Transpositions," C. S. Lewis, in the manner of Plato, spins a modern-day Allegory of the Cave to help his audience understand the true relationship and distinction between earth and heaven. In the allegory, or fable as Lewis calls it, a pregnant woman is thrown into a dark, high-walled dungeon with only a small window in the ceiling to permit in the rays of the sun. Several months later, she gives birth to a son who grows up in the dungeon and is thus never vouchsafed even a glimpse of the world outside his prison walls. Luckily, however, the woman was able to take with her into the dungeon a set of pencils and a wad of paper on which she has, for many years, drawn pictures of that greater world outside which her son has never seen and can hardly imagine really exists.

With her pencil she attempts to show him what fields, rivers, mountains, cities, and waves on a beach are like. He is a dutiful boy and he does his best to believe her when she tells him that this outer world is far more interesting and glorious than anything in the dungeon. At times he succeeds. On the whole he gets on tolerably well until, one day, he says something that gives his mother pause. For a minute or two they are at cross-purposes. Finally it dawns on her that he has, all these

years, lived under a misconception. "But," she gasps, "you
didn't think that the real world was full of lines drawn in
lead pencil?" "What?" asks the boy. "No pencil marks
there?" And instantly his whole notion of the outer
world becomes a blank. For the lines, by which alone he
was imagining it, have now been denied of it. He has no
idea of that which will exclude and dispense with the
lines, that of which the lines were merely a transposition.

The child, in short, has no idea that the lines he has interpreted as
reality are but a bare facsimile of the real fields and mountains and cities
of which the lines are merely a dim copy. Similarly, we who live on this
earth often imagine heaven as but the projection of a sketchy wish fulfillment, when, in fact, all the wishes we have ever wished and all the
dreams we have ever dreamed are but shadows of that greater outside
reality that is heaven. That is not to say that the dreams are bad or that
they need necessarily lead us astray, but that at some point they must be
surrendered to and absorbed by heaven like a candle flame that is over-
whelmed rather than extinguished by the risen sun.

Lewis means his fable to be, in part, an anti-Freudian allegory, and
it works as such. But here, at the conclusion of my book, I offer it instead
as a metaphor for our modern and postmodern world. For we are all like
the child in the fable, taught to believe and rest our hope in the paltry,
two-dimensional materialism of modernity or in the starved and bank-
rupt relativism of postmodernity, each of which only scratch the surface
of who we are, of what our universe is, and of what our destiny shall be.
If we are to regain our way and our sense of what is really real and truly
true, then we must, like the boy in Lewis's allegory, have some of our
most cherished assumptions smashed to bits. I have attempted in chapters 2–6, with the help of Lewis Agonistes, to wrestle and defeat some of
the key assumptions that our age has too quickly accepted as the truth:
that the nature of reality is down to up and that the material is all that
there is; that the close links between the myths of the ancient world and
the gospel of Christ prove that Christianity is only a fable with no historical basis in fact; that we have the power to build a utopia from which
ignorance, poverty, evil, and pain can be excluded; that there are no

absolutes and that the slippery nature of language renders all literature, including the Bible, ultimately meaningless; that hell is a violation of the dignity and equality of man and that heaven is nothing more than a mercenary wish fulfillment.

These and many other assumptions have served as our opponents in the arena of the twenty-first century, and I trust that, even if you have not learned how to wrestle with them, that you have at least come to recognize them *as* assumptions with no more final validity than the pencil lines drawn by Lewis's overeager mother. If this book has helped you to see past those lines toward greater possibilities, then it has served its purpose.

The legacy of C. S. Lewis is an extensive one, and it would be a difficult task to reduce that legacy to a single contribution. But if I were forced to do so, then I would have to reply that the greatest gift Lewis bequeathed to our age was simply that he taught us to see and to hear: to see all those hidden presuppositions that exert such an influence on us for good or for ill; to see the magic and the wonder that runs rampant in God's sympathetic universe; to hear the true story that the myths and the legends and the fairy tales have been telling us for thousands of years; to hear the voice of the great Bridegroom who is Christ calling to his beloved to rest in him. I am a man of many words and of many thoughts, and I have been known to speak at length on almost any topic. But when I read the works of Lewis, I find myself strangely stilled. At times I can almost hear him saying to me what Frank the Cabby says to the frantic Uncle Andrew in *The Magician's Nephew*, as Uncle Andrew continues to ramble on even as the land of Narnia is being called into life right before his eyes:

"Oh stow it, Guv'nor, do stow it . . . Watchin' and listenin' 's the thing at present; not talking."